FIRST RIGHTS

A Guide to Legal Rights For Young People

Maggie Rae, Patricia Hewitt and Barry Hugill

Illustrations by Corinne Pearlman

National Council for Civil Liberties 1986

National Council for Civil Liberties,
21 Tabard Street,
London SE1 4LA

Note

The law is different in Scotland and Northern Ireland. This book only deals
with England and Wales. At the end of the book, we give some useful books
and addresses of organisations which can help. Although all details in this
book are correct at the time of going to press, the law on certain points is
subject to change.

Acknowledgements for the first edition

The authors would like to express their heartfelt thanks to all those who have
helped in the preparation of this book and especially Jenny Levin, Tess Gill,
Joe Gill, Tom Gill, Larry Grant, Anna Coote, Charles Foster, Peter Newell,
Nettie Pollard and Judith Edmunds.

British Library Cataloguing in Publication Data

Rae, Maggie
    First rights: a guide to legal rights for young people – 3rd ed
    1. Children – Legal status, laws etc. – Great Britain
    I. Title II. Hewitt, Patricia III. Hugill, Barry IV. National Council for
    Civil Liberties
    323.3'52'0941   KD735

ISBN 0-946088-15-2

PRINTED IN GREAT BRITAIN
by the Yale Press, London.

CONTENTS

JOIN NCCL!

The **National Council for Civil Liberties** has campaigned since 1934 to defend and extend freedom of speech and expression, and to protect the rights of individuals and minorities to equal treatment under just laws. NCCL advises people on their rights; takes cases to courts and tribunals; lobbies Parliament and Government; publishes pamphlets about people's rights; and organises campaigns for law reforms. Funded mainly by subscriptions and donations, NCCL is the largest independent organisation working for human rights in the United Kingdom.

You can get further details about individual membership or affiliation by organisations or groups from NCCL, 21 Tabard Street, London SE1 4LA.

INTRODUCTION

The purpose of this guide is to explain, as clearly and practically as possible, the way the law treats young people. We cannot tell you what to do or give you advice on personal problems. But we do believe that, in order for you to make decisions about your own life, you need the fullest possible information about how the law will affect you.

Laws change, as social conditions change, and the present state of the law is not fixed. Attitudes towards childhood and youth have changed dramatically over the centuries. In medieval and Tudor Britain, for instance, children and young people worked alongside their parents in the fields or were apprenticed at an early age to learn a craft, while boys from upper-class families were sent away to court for their training.

The idea of 'childhood' as a state entirely different from adulthood, demanding widespread special protection and carrying few if any responsibilities was developed later, initially in wealthier families who could afford not to have their young people working. In working-class families, of course, economic demands meant that children had to earn their living from a very early age and, up until only 100 years ago, children and teenagers were to be found working in the mines, in factories, as chimney-sweeps and on the streets.

In 1819, a law was passed preventing children under nine from working in mines or factories. In 1874, a minimum age of ten was set for most jobs. In addition to the rules governing the employment of school-students, the Factories Acts place restrictions on the hours worked by women and by young people up to the age of 18.

The 1918 Education Act established compulsory education up to the age of 14; the school-leaving age was lifted to 15 in 1947 and again to 16 in 1972. Raising the school-leaving age was designed to improve educational opportunities, particularly for less well-off children; it also had the effect of delaying further the arrival of legal adulthood.

There have been many changes in the law since the first edition of this book was published in 1979. The courts have decided that children under 16 who have reached a 'sufficient understanding and intelligence' are capable of making up their own minds on medical treatment and in particular a girl can receive contraceptive advice and treatment without her parents consent. Another major change, the abolition of corporal punishment in schools, is to come into force in August 1987, after over 300 years of campaigning against

1

it. In 1669 a boy presented a petition to Parliament on behalf of children asking to stop school beatings. On 22 July 1986 MPs in the House of Commons voted for abolition by a majority of one vote.

Another development in the past few years is the growth of self help groups for young people in care (National Association for Young People in Care and Black and in Care). We hope you'll be able to discuss your own situation, and the legal position, with sympathetic adults. But if you're isolated, we suggest you contact one of the organisations listed at the end of each chapter or at the end of this book. In particular, the Children's Legal Centre provides expert advice on many subjects covered in this book.

A note on the Third Edition

There have been so many changes in the law, especially with the Police and Criminal Evidence Act and the British Nationality Act, that this book has had to be completely revised and rewritten. The authors and publishers are particularly grateful for the research and revision by Mark Paterson, and for the advice and assistance of Betty Rubinstein, Isobel Reid and the Children's Legal Centre, Gertrude Cohn, Nettie Pollard, Tom Cowan, Bill Birtles, Corinne Sweet and John Myers.

1
YOU AND YOUR FAMILY

Courts

In this chapter, we sometimes mention 'the court', which may be asked to make a decision about you and your family. There are a number of courts which can be involved in family matters: for instance, the magistrates' court deals with couples who are separated and who disagree about how much maintenance should be paid or where the children should live. The divorce courts handle matters where people are getting divorced and, again, may have to make a decision about where the children should live. Ordinary County Courts can sometimes decide disputes about children. In rare cases, a child may be made a 'ward of court' (for instance, to prevent one parent taking the child out of the country), and this would be dealt with by the High Court. It would be a good idea to have one 'family court' to deal with most of these matters, but so far no government has been prepared to set this up, although there is continual pressure to do so.

3

Living with your parents

Until you are 18, you are still a 'minor' and the law treats you as incapable of looking after yourself on your own and making all your own decisions. Of course, as you get older, you are more able to decide things for yourself – particularly if you start work at 16 and support yourself. But while you are under 18, the law generally assumes that you are under the control of an adult or adults – usually your parents.

Your parents – or whichever adults have charge of you – are said to have *custody* of you. In practice, this means they have the legal right to decide where you go to school, what you wear, how much pocket-money you get, how you are punished and so on, as long as they do this in a way considered to be reasonable. If your parents are married to each other, the law presumes that both of them have joint custody of you. If they separate or do not look after you properly the courts can give custody of you to one or other of them, or to someone else, or the local authority can take you into care (this is explained in chapter 3).

If your parents were not married when you were born, and have not married since, then you are said to be 'illegitimate' – although the law makes very little distinction now between an 'illegitimate' and a 'legitimate' child, and social prejudices are also breaking down. The law says that the mother

The law says your parents have custody of you whilst you are under 18.

has custody of an illegitimate child: the father has no automatic right to have custody of the child, although he can apply to the court for custody (see page 10 for more on this).

Who pays for your keep

Your parents are responsible for maintaining you until you are 18. This applies even though they may not have custody of you. For instance, if you are living with your mother, your father still has to contribute towards your upkeep. If you are in the care of the local authority, the same applies and the court can order your parents to pay maintenance to the local authority for you.

If you get married before you reach the age of 18, then your parents are no longer responsible for maintaining you.

Neglect

If your parents fail to look after you properly or ill-treat you, a court can order that someone else should have custody of you. If this happens it is important to tell your solicitor, social worker or *guardian ad litem* (see p.39) whether you have an aunt or other relation who wants to look after you, even if only at weekends. They must come to court and say so, to make it clear it is a definite order.

At court your parents can be prosecuted for treating you cruelly or damaging your health. Alternatively, the local authority can decide to take you into care (see chapter 3). If you feel that you are being ill-treated by your parents, you can get advice and help from your local social services department, or from a friendly teacher or a lawyer (for instance, at a local law centre). It's best to seek advice rather than run away. If you feel that you are being pushed out on your own before you're ready or that no-one is taking proper care of you and you want somebody for support, then you can also talk to a teacher or local social services department about it.

Your name

If your parents were married when you were born, then you were probably given your father's surname. If your parents separate and your mother wants to change your surname, she has to get your father's consent first. If your parents weren't married when you were born, then you will probably have been given your mother's surname – unless your mother decided that she wanted you to have your father's surname and allowed it to be put on your birth certificate.

Until you are 16, your parents cannot change your name without your consent (for instance, if your mother is divorced from your father and wants you to take the name of her new husband). Once you are 18, you can change your name without getting your parent's agreement. You can do this quite simply, just by using whatever name you like: or you can swear a statutory declaration or change your name by deed poll (go to a solicitor for these). But you can't have your birth certificate changed.

Citizenship and Nationality

Citizenship and Nationality are important because they affect your rights and those of your parents to remain in the UK; to leave and to return; and to work. People who are citizens of the UK can enter and remain in the UK without any restriction and they cannot be deported. Otherwise you need permission to enter and remain in the UK. Such permission can and usually is qualified, for example, the permission may be limited to staying for a certain length of time only, or granted only on condition that you do not work.

Born in the UK?

If you were born in the UK *before* the 1st January 1983 you will be a British citizen, regardless of the citizenship of your parents.

If you were born *after* 1st January 1983 you will only be a British citizen at birth if one of your parents is either a British citizen or lawfully settled in the UK – "parents" here includes your mother whether you are legitimate or illegitimate but your father only if you are legitimate.

This law, which came into force on the 1st January 1983, replaced the existing law which provided that anyone born in the UK or one of the colonies (Gibraltar, Hong Kong, or the Falkland Islands) was a UK citizen whatever their parents' nationality. Many children and young people who would previously have had UK citizenship will not now be entitled to it. Also the new law can make it more difficult for you to prove that you are a British national, as you may have to show not only your birth certificate but also give evidence as to your parents' citizenship or their lawful status in this country. These changes in the law mean that you can be a British citizen when your parents and some, or all, of your brothers or sisters are not, and vice versa. This has led to cases of families being split up.

If you were born in the UK and are not a British citizen you will not need permission to stay here but if you leave, for example, to go on holiday, you will need permission to re-enter the country on your return.

If your parents have been granted permission to stay here for a particular length of time, then you will usually be granted permission to stay for the same length of time, the same way that if your parents apply for British citizenship and are accepted, then you will probably also be accepted.

Coming to join your family in the UK?

Many parents, when coming to live in this country, leave their children, wife and members of the family in their country of origin until they have become established in the UK.

If you are under 18 years old and apply to join your parent or parents in the UK you may be allowed to do so. However, before coming to the UK you will have to apply for permission from the Home Office. This is a lengthy and distressing process, during which you and your family members can expect to be subjected to lengthy questioning by Home Office officials who will be concerned to ensure that you and your family are not lying about your membership of the family. If your family come from the Indian Subcontinent, the Home Office are likely to be particularly difficult as they believe that some families try and bring in the children of friends and relatives as their own.

In these interviews each person will be interviewed separately although if you are under 14 years old you must be questioned in the presence of an adult member of your family. If answers given by family members are inconsistent with each other then your application for entry will be delayed until discrepancies are sorted out. If these cannot be explained you will probably be refused permission to settle here.

If you are planning to come and live with only one of your parents in this country, for example, if your parents are separated, then your parent must show either that s/he has had sole responsibility for your upbringing or that there are serious or compelling family or other reasons which make it desirable to allow you to come and live here. These rules have been applied very harshly so that children have been refused entry even though their parent has paid for their upbringing.

Monica Pinnock, a 14-year-old Jamaican, living with her mother and stepfather in their grossly overcrowded two-roomed house was refused settlement. Monica shared a bed with her stepbrothers, aged 18 and 15 and her stepsister aged 11. There was some suggestion that Monica had been ill-treated by her mother and she had a difficult relationship with her stepfather who was irregularly employed in poorly paid jobs and who resented her presence in the household. Her sponsoring father was married, living in the UK in comfortable well-maintained accommodation. The Home Office suggested that Monica was "probably better off" in familiar surroundings in Jamaica. According to the adjudicator hearing the appeal, it was not enough "to say that the appellant has to share a bed with a 17-year-old half brother . . . it has to be shown that this is an unavoidable situation, incapable of being remedied by reasonable efforts on the part of the appellant's parents." He therefore upheld the Home Office refusal for settlement.

Recently a 17-year-old Hungarian boy, **Balazs Nemeny** was likewise at first refused permission to remain in the UK with his political refugee mother and stepfather. Balazs's father in Hungary is a strict Communist. Balazs himself has liberal leanings. The adjudicator accepted that Balazs, who overstayed the leave permitted by the Hungarian authorities, would suffer some penalty on his return – "probably a few months in a labour camp'". Further, the adjudicator commented, "If he returns it is likely that he will have to suppress his views, otherwise he will be frozen out of any worthwhile job and possibly suffer worse. In short, he must either change his views completely or live a lie for the rest of his life". Even so, to the adjudicator, these were not sufficiently compelling considerations but, following representations, the Secretary of State exercised his discretion to allow Balazs to remain in the U.K.

What were the differences between these two cases? Why do you think Balazs Nemeny was finally allowed to stay in the UK while Monica Pinnock wasn't?

Coming to join your adopted family in the UK?

Special rules apply to children who have been adopted abroad and now wish to settle with their adopted parents in the UK.

You don't have to have been legally adopted to qualify for entry but the relationship between you and your "adopted" parents must have some legal force in your country of origin. You will be allowed to join your adopted parents only if the Home Office is satisfied that there has been "a genuine transfer of parental responsibility on the grounds of the original parents' incapacity to care for the children" and your adoption was not simply done to help you gain entry into the country.

It is unlikely that this condition will be satisfied if you have continued to live with your parents after being adopted. The Home Office have also excluded children who were genuinely adopted where their natural parents could or would have been capable of caring for them.

14-year-old **Asuncion Evangelista** was adopted by her natural aunt when she was five years old. Asuncion's biological parents were very poor; they had seven children and lived in a one-room house in the Philippines; her biological father suffered from pulmonary tuberculosis. The tribunal refused her entry because while "there is evidence of poverty and overcrowding in the home of the natural parents . . . there is nonetheless evidence that the parents have had the ability to care for six other children, three of whom were born after the applicant. All the applicant's brothers and sisters have remained at home and have been brought up by their natural parents. As they have been able to care, not only for the applicant's three elder brothers but also for the younger children, it does not seem logical to the tribunal to find, in the absence of evidence relating peculiarly to the applicant, that they were unable to give similar care to her".

Nationality law is complicated and if you are doubtful about your position or that of your family you should get expert advice.

Religion

You can't stop your parents making you a member of any particular faith or going through formal ceremonies such as baptism. Your parents can insist on you having religious instruction if you live at home, and you have no legal right to prevent this. It is also possible for one of your parents to alter your religion without your consent – for instance if there is a dispute about which religion you should take, or if your parents divorce – although the court can take your views into account if they think you are old enough. The court may also stop you being brought up in a particular religion if they think this would be bad for you.

If you are going to a state school, the law says you should have religious instruction unless your parents withdraw you from these classes. You have no right yourself to withdraw from religious instruction, but, if you want to, you can ask your parents to withdraw you.

Medical treatment

Normally, your parents will arrange for you to see the doctor if you are ill or need a check-up. If you have to go to hospital, they will have to sign a

8

consent form before you can have an operation or certain other kinds of treatment.

When you are 16 you can consent to or withhold consent to medical and dental treatment, independently of your parents. If you are under 16, and able to consent to treatment, that is the doctor thinks that you understand the implications of the proposed treatment, then you can consent to the treatment independently of your parents. The doctor may feel it desirable to involve your parents, and urge you to speak to them – particularly if you are requesting contraception. Doctors should not however breach your confidence by telling your parents about the consultation. However the General Medical Council has said that in certain circumstances, if doctors believe it to be in your medical interests, then they may inform your parents about the consultation. This situation has not been resolved.

The recent court case brought by Mrs Gillick was intended to establish that doctors must tell your parents before giving you advice or treatment in relation to contraception or abortion, and also implied the same for certain other forms of medical treatment. The House of Lords rejected Mrs Gillick's case, but the DHSS has now reviewed and revised its guidance to doctors and other health service workers in relation to contraceptive advice and treatment to young people under 16. In particular, doctors and other health workers are advised to take special care not to undermine parental responsibility and family stability – they should persuade the young person to tell the parents or guardian, or to let the doctor inform them, of any advice or treatment given. They are also advised that it should be most unusual to provide contraceptive advice or treatment to under-16s without parental knowledge or consent. Doctors and other health professionals would be justified in giving advice and treatment without parental knowledge and consent in some specified exceptional cases, such as:-

> when family relationships have broken down;
> when the young person was mature enough to understand the moral, social and emotional implications;
> when the person could not allow the parents to know;
> when the young person is likely to begin or to continue having sex with or without contraception;
> when the person's mental or physical health is liable to suffer without advice or treatment;
> or where it is deemed to be in the child's best interests.

Where it is felt that parents are not acting in the child's best interests in consenting to or withholding consent for other types of medical treatment, it is possible to stop the treatment or have it altered by having the child made a 'ward of court' – which means that the court takes over the legal powers of the parents. For instance, an educational psychologist took legal proceedings in 1975 to prevent a handicapped 11-year-old girl being sterilized: the girl was made a ward of court and the court decided that the operation was not in the girl's interests and it refused its consent. The courts have also ordered blood transfusions where these have been opposed by parents on religious grounds.

Travelling and getting a passport

You can travel with either of your parents on their passports, if your name is officially entered on them, until you are 16. After that (or if you are younger and you are travelling without a parent) you will need your own passport. Your parents must apply for a passport on your behalf until you reach 18 when you can get your own passport without your parent's consent. If you are going abroad on a school trip, the school will probably get a group passport for all of you. On some day-trips to Europe you don't need a passport at all.

If you were born abroad, or if your parents are not UK citizens, then you may have a passport from a different country. If not, you could apply for a passport to the High Commission of the country which claims you as a citizen.

Punishment

Parents have the legal right to decide how you should be punished. They are allowed to use corporal punishment – which usually just means a slap for a young child. But if your parents hit you too severely, they can be prosecuted for assault. The court would then have to decide whether the punishment was 'moderate and reasonable', depending on how old and how strong you are. If your parents hit you excessively, you should get help from a friendly teacher, or the local social services department can take you into care if the circumstances are serious enough.

If your parents separate, who will look after you?

If your parents separate or decide to get divorced, they may disagree about whether you should live with your father or your mother. If this happens, a court has to decide which parent you will live with. This will usually either be a magistrate's court or a county court if your parents are separating but not getting divorced, or a divorce county court or the High Court if they are getting a divorce.

When a court decides who is to have custody of you, it must first decide what would be best for you. It should take your views into account, although this will depend on your age and how well-thought-out the court thinks you are. Usually, very young children stay with their mother. It is quite rare for a father to get custody if he has never been married to the mother: but this might happen if your mother had neglected you, or was in prison, or for some reason the court thought she was quite unsuitable to look after you.

If your parents are in dispute about who should have custody of you and any brothers or sisters you may have, you may get a visit from a social worker who will then report back to the court. You should see the social worker by yourself, and explain as clearly as you can what you think you would like best.

The County Court and the High Court can ask the Official Solicitor – who is a lawyer working for the court – to represent you if your parents disagree about custody. The Official Solicitor should make a thorough investigation into the case and talk to you, and will then normally prepare a report for the court setting out the details of the investigations.

It is very unlikely that you and your brothers or sisters will be split up. Usually, the court will decide to award both 'custody' and 'care and control' to one parent. 'Custody' means the right to take important decisions about your life, such as what school you go to, what religion you belong to, what medical treatment you have and so on (as we explained earlier on page 8); 'care and control' means the day-to-day responsibility of looking after you. Occasionally the court may award 'custody' to both your parents, who should then consult each other about the decisions on important matters, while giving 'care and control' to the parent you will be living with.

Usually the court will say that the parent you are not living with should have 'access' to you i.e. the right to see you regularly. The court may say when and where this should happen (e.g. every other weekend) or it may leave things flexible. The court order is not necessarily 'for ever' and can be varied subsequently if circumstances change.

Fostering

You may be looked after by 'foster parents' – people who aren't your natural parents, but who take you into their family. Your parents might, for instance, decide to have you fostered if they didn't want you adopted but couldn't look after you themselves – possibly because your mother is in hospital, or because they can't find a home for the family. Foster parents don't take over the legal rights and responsibilities of your natural parents, so that your parents still have to make the decisions about where you go to school and so on.

You may be placed with foster parents by the local authority after you have been taken into care. If this happens, then the local authority takes on the legal powers of your natural parents and the authority (i.e. the social workers looking after you) will make the decisions about your schooling, religion, medical treatment etc. The local authority is responsible for making sure that your foster parents look after you properly. More about care in chapter 3.

Foster parents can apply for a custodianship order if you have lived with them for 3 years, or 12 months if the person who has custody of you agrees to the order being made. If an order is made, then you cannot be taken away from your foster parents without the court's agreement.

Adoption

About 500,000 people in this country (including adults) were adopted as children. Some people don't discover that they are adopted until they reach their teens – and a few people may never be told. Other children are told that they are adopted as soon as they are old enough to understand.

Being adopted means that your new, adoptive parents take over all the legal rights and responsibilities of your parents: in law, your adopters become your parents.

Adopted children usually have their surname changed when they are adopted, to that of their adoptive parents. After an adoption order is made you will be given a new birth certificate.

Once you have been adopted any links with your natural parents will usually be ended completely. Nowadays, some adopted children do retain some contact with their natural families. But where this occurs it is normally very limited.

In some cases, however, your mother and her new husband may have adopted you jointly: so that your adoptive mother is also your real mother.

The law recognises that many adoptive children want to know who their real parents were, or may even want to go and see their natural father or mother. Once you reach the age of 18, you have the right to see your birth record which will tell you the name of one or both of your natural parents. You should apply to the Registrar of Births, Deaths and Marriages, 10 Kingsway, London WC2 (01-242 0262) or at the local registry office (in the phone book).

If you were adopted before 12 November 1975, you have to have an interview with a counsellor provided by the registrar's department before you will be shown your birth records. If you were adopted after that date, it is up to you whether you see the counsellor.

You can only be adopted on the order of a court, and your natural parents have the right to object. The court can overrule their objections. When deciding whether or not to make an adoption order, the court has to give first consideration to the need to safeguard your well-being until you are an adult. If you were adopted when you were a baby or very young child, no-one will have asked you your opinion. But if you are adopted when you are older (and children can be adopted up to the age of 18), the court should find out what your wishes are and, as far as possible, take these into account.

Guardianship

Your parents and the courts have the power to appoint someone to be your guardian. Your parents may do this in their will, to make sure there is someone to look after you if they die. Normally, guardians are only appointed where your parents are dead or have deserted you. Your guardian will be the person who has custody of you, and usually has the power to administer your property, if you have any. Your guardian also has to consent to your marrying, if you are under 18. But your guardian must act in accordance with your best interests and can be removed or replaced by the courts.

Custodianship

This is a new type of order that the court can make which gives legal custody of you to someone other than your parents. The person with whom you are living can apply to the court for an order if you have lived with them for a total of 3 years including the three months immediately before they apply. If the person who has legal custody of you (usually your parent or parents) agrees to a custodianship order being made, the application can be made when you have lived with the person for a shorter period of time – 3 months if the person you live with is a relative or step-parent, or a year for someone who is not.

If a custodianship order is made then your custodian has all the rights and duties that your parents normally have. This law is supposed to help stop children who are looked after by relatives or foster parents being suddenly removed by their parents or the local authority.

Ward of court

Being made a ward of court usually only happens in an emergency – for instance, if your parents are separated or divorced, and your mother thinks your father will take you out of the country against your will and she has no other way of stopping him. (It could be the other way round, of course.) Or someone close to you (for instance, a teacher or welfare worker) can apply to have you made a ward of court if she or he thinks that your parents are making a decision which will be very bad for you (see page 11 for an example of this).

Local councils may also apply to have you made a ward of court in order to keep you in care, although it is more usual for them to apply for a care order (as explained on page 33-4). Also, if you are being looked after by a friend or relative they can apply to have you made a ward of court to ensure you are not removed from their care.

If you feel that no-one is taking notice of what you want when you are being made a ward of court, then you can contact the Official Solicitor – part of whose job is to help those who have difficulty getting themselves heard at court. The Official Solicitor has a policy that if you are 8 years of age or older, the court should consult you as to what you want and take your wishes seriously.

Your parents may appoint a guardian in their will to make sure there is someone to look after you if they die.

13

If you are made a ward of court, the court itself takes the place of your parents when it comes to making the main decisions about your life – what school you go to, where you live, what medical treatment you have, and so on. But you will go on living at home, unless the court decides that it would be better for you to be placed in the care of the local authority. If that happens, you would probably live in a community home or with foster parents (see page 30).

If you are a ward of court and want to marry before you reach 18, the court has to agree. This also applies if you want to leave the country.

Recently, a 15 year old girl managed to get herself made a ward of court because the parent with whom she did not want to live had been given custody of her after her parents' divorce. For this you would need help and advice from a solicitor experienced in these matters.

Leaving home

Most people leave home because they have a job and are earning enough to live independently, or they are going away to study. But problems can arise, either if you want to leave home before you're 18 and your parents don't want you to, or if you leave home without enough money or anywhere to go.

If your parents don't object to your leaving home before the age of 18, and you keep out of trouble, you shouldn't have any difficulties. But if they do object and ask the police to find you, or if you come to the attention of the social services department or the police, you may find yourself in front of the courts – even though you haven't broken the law. This is more likely to happen to a girl since, if you are sleeping with someone you're not married to, the police or social workers may decide you are in 'moral danger' and in need of 'care and control'.

If you are taken to court, your parents might have to promise the court to keep proper control over you, or the court may appoint a social worker to keep an eye on you. Or you may be placed in the care of the local authority (see chapter 3 for details).

You'll be less likely to end up in court if you have a job and can share accommodation with a friend of the same sex and generally give the appearance of leading a respectable life – and, of course, if you can avoid your parents complaining to the police. Things will be far more difficult if you are under 16, since you probably won't have a job or any income, and if you leave school to get a job you can be taken to court for not attending school.

Once you are 18, you can live where you like.

Many towns and cities have places where you can get advice – about where to live, the law and so on. There are some addresses at the end of the book, or you can ask the local Citizens' Advice Bureau.

2
SCHOOL

This chapter is an A to Z guide ('Attendance' to 'Uniform' anyway!) to how the law affects school-pupils and their parents. You can get more information from the books and organisations listed at the end of the book.

Attendance

Education is compulsory in this country from the age of five until 16. The local council (called the Local Education Authority or LEA) has to provide enough schools for the children in their area. Most children and young people go to schools run by the LEA, which are free, although some go to private schools where parents have to pay. If your parents don't send you to school at all, and the LEA finds out and thinks you are not getting a proper education, they can serve a notice on your parents requiring them to convince the LEA that you are being properly educated. If your parents satisfy the LEA, that will be the end of the matter.

If the LEA thinks that you should be going to school, they will tell your parents which school to send you to. If you still don't go, the LEA will probably send your parents a *school attendance order* naming the school you have to go to. Your parents can be taken to court if they don't obey the order, and if they are found guilty they can be fined up to £200.

See *Truanting* for what happens if you are sent to school, but don't turn up regularly, and *Leaving school* for when you can leave.

Changing things at school

If you have difficulty understanding a teacher or keeping up with the work, you should talk to your teacher about the difficulties. If a number of you are concerned about some aspect of the school – rules on uniform, for instance – you should get together to decide what to do. You might decide that you should all try and see the head-teacher, or if this doesn't work write a letter to the governors.

Your school may have a school council or some other democratic procedure which allows you to raise issues and have them discussed by pupils and teachers. If your school doesn't have one, you might talk to other students about pressing for a school council.

If your parents are worried about the education you are getting or the way the school is run, they should talk to the head-teacher. If they're still not happy, they could go to the school governors or managers (see under *Governors*) or to the local education authority (see under *LEA*).

Choosing a school

In some places, particularly in the country or a small town, there will only be one or two schools which you could go to. In a city, however, there may be a number of schools fairly near where you live. The LEA has to decide which school you will go to. They may consult your teacher (for instance, if you're moving from primary to secondary school). They must take your parents' wishes into account. But they don't have to ask you what you think.

If you feel strongly about which school you want to go to, or would like to find out more about the different schools available, you should tell your parents, who can go and visit the schools and see the head-teacher. Here are some questions which your parents could ask the head-teacher:

– How many pupils are there? (you or your parents may prefer a smaller school)
– What subjects are available? (for instance, what languages are provided?)
– Does the school timetable allow you to combine a variety of subjects, for instance science/languages/history?
– How does the school deal with 'girls' subjects' and 'boys' subjects'? Does everyone have to do both (for instance, domestic science and metal work)? Does the school encourage girls to choose only 'girls' subjects' and boys to choose only 'boys' subjects'?
– Are there adequate facilities for children with disabilities?
– What are the school rules? (for instance, concerning uniform)
– Is there any rule forbidding pupils participating in political activities outside school hours?
– Is there a school council or any other way in which pupils can jointly raise issues with teachers?

Obviously, there are plenty of other questions to be asked, depending on your particular interests and preferences.

Once you and your parents have decided which school you most want to go to, they should notify the LEA. The LEA will try to send you to that school, but they don't have to if the school is full, or outside the area where you live, or if they think it is too far away or unsuitable for any other reason. You have the best chance of going to the school of your choice if you already have a brother or sister there, or if your parents have chosen it for religious reasons, or because they particularly want a single-sex or co-educational school, or because it provides special facilities which you need (e.g. if you are physically handicapped, or if you have a particular talent for which the school provides).

If you are refused a place at the school you have chosen, your parents will be able to appeal.

Some parents who can afford it make sure their child gets into the school they want by moving into the area covered by the school. Others feel that the best thing to do is to get involved in the Parent-Teachers Association, become active in school affairs and try to make the school work the way they want. Occasionally, parents who feel very strongly about which school their child should go to, refuse to send the child to school until they get their way. Sometimes they succeed, but they may be served with a school attendance order (see page 15) ordering them to follow the LEA's decision.

16

If your parents decide to send you to a private, fee-paying school, then the choice of school is up to them, provided, of course, that the school has a vacancy and you meet the entrance requirements.

Department of Education and Science (DES)

The DES is the government department which has the overall responsibility for making sure that schools are provided throughout England and Wales.

The DES is responsible to a Cabinet Minister, the Secretary of State for Education. In some cases, the Secretary of State can deal with an appeal by parents against the LEA's decision not to send their child to the school they want, or a decision to suspend or expel a child. The DES cannot control what subjects are taught in schools, or how they are taught. (Only religious instruction and physical education are compulsory). But they send inspectors to schools to make sure that the standard of work is satisfactory.

The DES is at Elizabeth House, York Road, London, SE1 (01-928 9222).

Disabilities: children and young people.

One in ten people in this country has a disability. Many more children with these special problems to overcome – deafness, partial sight or whatever – should be educated in mainstream, that is, ordinary, schools. When special schools were first introduced they were an improvement on what went before and they are still essential for some. If you feel you can be satisfactorily educated in an ordinary school but are in a special school, you can enquire about changing, though it may not be easy to bring this about. Depending on the area you live in, the LEA should be helpful, as they have an obligation to consider this.

The LEA has to make special provision to meet the particular needs of some children, for instance:
– special schools for blind, deaf or handicapped children;
– special classes or schools for children with learning difficulties;
– home tuition for children who cannot get to school or who would find it embarrassing to attend. This could apply to a pregnant schoolgirl, or to someone who has been suspended and who doesn't have a place at another school.

LEAs also have to identify children who have special educational needs and assess what they are. The LEAs must ensure that children with special needs are educated with children without special needs.

Parents should be consulted about any decision to classify their child as 'educationally subnormal' and in need of special education. If they disagree with the decision, they can appeal against it, and can get advice from the Advisory Centre for Education (address at the end of the book).

All young people have the right to education until their 19th birthday. But some LEAs will let young people with special needs continue after they are 19. You can ask about this. Some LEAs also offer link courses with a local college of further education whilst you are still at school. Link courses can be a good way of finding out about the range of courses offered at college.

Many Further Education Colleges (also known as Technical Colleges) now offer a range of courses for people with special needs, as well as providing a wide range of courses on all subjects. You can usually study part-time or full-time. Some colleges also offer courses in basic living skills; mobility and independence training or the opportunity to take other public examinations for business or technical qualifications. If you want more information you can contact the National Children's Bureau (address at the end of the book).

Discipline

The head-teacher is responsible for discipline in the school. So s/he can decide on the rules which you have to obey. The rules can say what you have to wear to school, whether or not you can smoke, whether any particular shops are out of bounds, what punishments can be imposed if you break the rules, and so on. In one court case, the court decided that it was perfectly all right for pupils to be ordered to run errands for the teachers.

The rules can also be used to forbid you getting involved in any political activity at school – or distributing their literature. Some schools have stopped pupils distributing National Front literature.

Head-teachers are also allowed to make rules about what you do outside school. They can forbid you to smoke, even if your parents don't mind. This kind of rule has also been upheld by the courts.

The head-teacher may consult the teachers and governors before making the rules. Some schools have councils, which give pupils a say in making the rules. But it is up to the head-teacher whether or not you are allowed to have a school council.

You and your parents can ask for a copy of the school rules. But you don't have any legal right to see them. Workers in a factory or office do have a legal right to see rules made by the employer, and there is a Government Code about these rules. Should there perhaps also be a Government Code on school rules?

Discrimination

It is unlawful for a school or an LEA to treat you unfairly because of your race or sex. Single-sex schools are still allowed, but the LEA must make sure that, overall, girls and boys get the same educational provision within the LEA's area.

Here are some examples of unlawful sex discrimination:
- Refusing to let girls do woodwork, technical drawing or engineering because they are 'boys' subjects'.
- Refusing to let boys do cooking, sewing or home economics because they are 'girls' subjects'.
- Saying that you can only do technical drawing if you have previously done metalwork. (Since hardly any girls do metalwork, this rule in effect discriminates against girls by preventing most of them from doing technical drawing).
- Giving different punishments for boys and girls, such as caning for boys and detention for girls.
- Applying a quota to the numbers of each sex who can enter the school.
- Providing different facilities for boys and girls to do gym. But schools are

18

allowed to discriminate when it comes to sport, by banning girls from, say, football and cricket.

Unlawful race discrimination includes applying a quota to the numbers of pupils from different racial groups who can come to the school. 'Bussing' children from one area to another in order to get a 'racial balance' in each school is also unlawful. Treating children of any particular race less favourably is unlawful.

If you think your school or LEA is discriminating unfairly, you or your parents should raise it with the teachers. The head may decide that the situation should be changed. You can get the Equal Opportunities Commission, the Commission for Racial Equality or NCCL to help (addresses at the end of book). If this doesn't work, they can help your parents to take the LEA or school to court.

It is unlawful for a school to treat you unfairly because of your sex.

Expulsion

You should only be expelled if you do something very seriously wrong. If your parents think the decision to expel you was wrong, they can appeal to the Secretary of State for Education. (The Advisory Centre for Education can advise on this.)

But if you are expelled from one school, and you are under 16, the LEA either has to find you another school or arrange for you to be educated in some other way, for instance by providing a home tutor. In practice, it may be some time before other arrangements are made.

Private schools (dealt with below) make their own rules about expulsion.

Free Schools

Free schools have been set up in a few places, as an alternative to conventional education. Some are private schools which don't charge a fee. Others are supported by Local Educational Authorities. Some parents choose to send their children there, because they object to the education provided in other schools.

An LEA may send a persistent truant to a free school in the hope that s/he will do better there. Free schools allow pupils more choice in what they do, and encourage children to make their own decisions and rules instead of having to obey someone else's rules. You can get more information about free schools from *Education Otherwise,* 4 Coombe Gardens, New Malden, Surrey. Tel: 01-942 0286.

Governors

Every state school must have a board of governors. Some schools may be grouped together to share one lot of governors.

Each board of governors has a list of Articles which set out the different responsibilities of the LEA, the governors and the head-teacher.

In most schools, governors are involved in choosing (or sacking) the head-teacher, deputy heads and teachers; fixing holiday dates; deciding how the school spends its money; and deciding whether to suspend or expel a pupil.

Governors are appointed by the LEA and usually include a number of people connected with local politics. Schools must have parent governors and teacher representatives. A few have pupil governors although there are legal difficulties in appointing a governor under 18 if the governors have financial responsibilities for the school. A committee on school governors recommended that all governors should include representatives of the parents and staff.

How much the governors get involved in the school depends very much on the interest they show and the extent to which the head-teacher tries to involve them.

You probably won't see much of your school governors, except on occasional visits or at assemblies or speech-days. But if you have an important complaint about the running of the school (for instance, sex or race discrimination) and the head-teacher hasn't convinced you there's a good reason for the situation or hasn't dealt with your complaint, you may want to bring it to the attention of the governors. If you can find out who the parents' representative on the board of governors is, ask him or her to raise it. Otherwise, ask the school or the local town hall for the name and address of the chair of the governors and write to him or her.

Health service

All LEAs have a school health service which is now run by the National Health Service. It organises regular, compulsory medical inspections at school. If your parents don't let you go, they can be fined. They also provide dentists, and special clinics if you have special problems (such as bedwetting, or if you seem to be emotionally disturbed).

Homework

Most secondary schools and some junior schools set homework. There are arguments for and against homework, although obviously it's bad if you're set too much and can't do it in the time available. The law is very unclear about whether or not you can be forced to do it or punished if you don't. In one case, a court decided it was unlawful for a teacher to punish a pupil for failing to do his homework. But this probably only applies to junior schools. It seems likely that secondary schools have a legal right to set homework and to punish you if you don't do it.

Inspectors

Some inspectors are employed by the Department of Education and Science which is a national government department (see *DES*). Others work for the LEA. The inspectors make regular checks on schools and are mainly concerned with the standard of work being done in the school. They can advise teachers about teaching methods, subjects and curriculum. If they feel a school is being very badly run, they may report this to the DES or the LEA who can decide what action to take.

Local Education Authority (LEA)

There are 104 LEAs in England and Wales which are responsible for providing educational facilities in their areas. In London, the Inner London Education Authority is responsible for providing facilities for all the inner London boroughs. Each LEA is run by the Chief Education Officer, who is responsible to the local council's Education Committee which consists of elected councillors.

LEAs are responsible for providing adequate facilities for education and sport, although what is considered adequate varies from area to area.

21

The LEA has to provide enough schools for each area. They may also be responsible for organising special schools for children and young people with disabilities; transport to and from schools; providing playing fields; and running the careers service.

The LEA is not directly involved in the running of your school. This is done by the governors and the head-teacher.

Leaving school

Education is compulsory from the age of five until 16. But you can't actually leave school on your 16th birthday. A set of rules decides the date when you can actually leave. These are as follows:

1. If your birthday is between 1 September and 31 January, you can't leave school until the end of the spring term following your birthday.

2. If your birthday is between 31 January and the Friday before the last Monday in May, you can't leave school until that Friday (this is called the May school leaving date).

3. If your birthday is between the May school leaving date and 1 September, you can also leave on the May school leaving date.

Meals

The LEA used to have to run a school meals service providing a mid-day meal for all the pupils at their schools. Now however it only has to make such provision as it sees fit. The result is that the food provided at school varies greatly from area to area: some LEAs provide hot meals and some only snacks and then only for children whose parents are on supplementary benefit or on low incomes. A charge is made although families on low income can apply for free meals (see *Money*). The government decides how much should be charged, but an LEA can decide to spend more than that on each meal. School meals used to be free for all pupils, and ought to be made free again.

Money

Your parents may be able to get money from the LEA for:
– your school uniform and other essential clothing;
– maintenance for you if you stay on after 16;
– transport to and from school (see also *Transport,* page 25);
– boarding school fees, if boarding is the only way you can get a proper education because of special needs etc. or because your parents are in the forces or diplomatic service abroad.

They may also be able to claim free meals for you.

Most LEAs have a scheme for giving School Uniform Grants to parents of secondary school children. Some LEAs use the same income figures as they use for free school meals for working out whether or not you qualify. Others are meaner, and use lower income limits. Some LEAs give cash, others give vouchers for use at shops selling uniforms.

If your parents are on supplementary benefit, they should certainly be able to get a uniform grant. They should apply first to the local education council and then, if they're refused, apply to the social security office and tell them that the council have turned down the application. Sometimes the council and the social security office disagree about whose responsibility it is to pay for clothing and uniforms. A lot of LEAs have a limited budget for uniform grants and this tends to get used up very quickly, so it's a good idea to get your parents to claim early in the year.

Some LEAs provide Educational Maintenance Allowances (EMAs) to the parents of children who stay on after the school leaving age. These are discretionary. If you think you might be eligible, ask your LEA for details.

The head-teacher of your school may also be able to find money to pay for special provisions e.g. hire of a musical instrument.

If you or your parents want to find out more about education grants you should contact the LEA (look in the phone book under the name of your council, or ask at the town hall). It's a good idea to apply early in the year, before the LEA's money runs out.

If your parents are claiming supplementary benefit or family income supplement you will be entitled to free school meals. But you still have to fill in an application form, which you get at the education office, town hall or social security office. In April 1988, supplementary benefit will be replaced by income support, and family income supplement by family credit. Only those on income support will be entitled to free school meals.

Private schools

Your parents can decide to have you educated privately, in a fee-paying school. Strangely enough, the posh private schools are called public schools.

You and your parents should look at the school prospectus and rules, and any other information you can get, to find out what the school views are on uniform, punishment and so on, and what kind of subjects and facilities they provide.

Your parents can complain to the Secretary of State for Education if they think the school premises are unsuitable, or if the proprietor or any teacher is unfit for the post.

Most children are educated in state schools. Most of this chapter does not apply to private schools.

Punishment

'Corporal punishment' means any form of punishment where the teacher hits you, whether by hand or with a cane, belt, ruler, book or any other instrument. The UK is the only EEC country which still lets teachers hit children. According to our law, corporal punishment has to be 'reasonable and moderate', but British courts are very lenient towards teachers and have often ruled even very severe beatings to be both reasonable and moderate.

Corporal punishment has been banned by many LEAs, and most others have rules restricting its use, but teachers often ignore them. In England and Wales all instances of corporal punishment must be written down in a book, but again this is often ignored. Contact STOPP – the Society of Teachers Opposed to Physical Punishment – for details of local rules.

In February 1982 the European Court of Human Rights ruled that pupils must not be given corporal punishment if their parents object. The government has since decided that corporal punishment in schools is to be abolished and this is now part of the Education Bill going through parliament at the end of 1986. If the Bill is passed then, corporal punishment in schools will be illegal from August 1987. However, if you are at a private school, teachers will still be allowed to hit you, unless your fees are paid out of public money i.e. a local authority grant. But, if you are a privately-funded student, any breach of the European Court's ruling would still be very serious and if your parents write to your school objecting to corporal punishment you are almost certainly safe from it. A form for your parents to do this is available free of charge from STOPP.

If you or your parents want to complain about a beating you have received, contact STOPP, who will help you. If you have marks or bruises, you should *immediately:*
* get someone to take photographs of the injuries
* be examined by a doctor

If you want to take legal action you should go immediately to the nearest police station with your parents and make a formal complaint of assault.

The moves to stop physical punishment of young people in schools may have an effect on the way young people are treated at home – already many social services departments prohibit foster parents from using physical punishment, and parents in general aren't allowed to do what they wish to you as much as they used to be.

Religion

Your school has to run a morning assembly so that all the pupils can join in what the law calls 'collective worship'. The school must also run religious education lessons. The assembly doesn't have to be Church of England, or even Christian, and some schools try to run an assembly which people of many different religions can join in. The LEA can arrange for you to have different religious education from the course usually taught at your school: this can be done at your own school, or at a different school provided it doesn't interfere with your other lessons.

Your parents can withdraw you from religious instruction and morning prayers, by writing to the head-teacher. But you don't have any right yourself to withdraw from religious instruction or worship.

School records and reports

Most schools send parents a regular report on their child's progress.

In addition, schools keep secret records about their pupils. Not all schools keep the same kind of reports and the quality and form they take varies greatly from LEA to LEA. Some include your photograph as well as details about your academic progress and information about your behaviour, appearance, family and friends. Sometimes this information is recorded not in words but in points (e.g. you will be rated 0 to 10 for 'honesty', 'leadership' etc) to make it look more scientific.

There are no legal controls on the keeping of school records or who sees them except under the Data Protection Act, for computerised records. Neither you nor your parents have any legal right to see them, although they may be shown to a large number of other people – including a new school, an educational welfare officer, social worker, probation officer or even the police. The records may also form the basis for a reference given by your school to a prospective employer or college. If you are taken to court, the LEA may have to provide a report on you to the court, and may do so by basing it on your school record.

School records are meant to give teachers full information about pupils so that they can do their job properly. But some records contain inaccurate, irrelevant or out-of-date information. NCCL and the Advisory Centre for Education want to see these records opened to parents and pupils aged 16 or over. A few LEAs have decided to show school records (although not confidential medical or psychiatric reports) to parents. These include ILEA (primary schools only), Manchester, Clwyd and Gwent.

Subjects

The head-teacher has the right to decide what subjects are taught at your school. S/he will usually consult with the LEA and the other teachers – but it is most unlikely that anyone will ask you for your views. The head-teacher also decides on the timetable, which of course can restrict the actual choice of subjects open to you.

If you want to do a subject which your school doesn't provide, you should ask the head-teacher whether arrangements could be made, for instance by sending you to another school for that subject. If two subjects you want to do (e.g. metalwork and home economics) are timetabled at the same time, you should also ask the teacher and the head to reconsider their decision. But if they don't change the timetable, all you can really do is get your parents to try and transfer you to a school which can meet your needs better.

Suspension

Suspension is increasingly used as a punishment. It means that you are temporarily banned from the school. Normally you should be suspended only if there is a serious reason. The head-teacher usually makes the decision, although in some areas the head cannot suspend you unless s/he gets the governors' consent. In some schools, you have the right to appeal to the governors against the decision to suspend you. You should ask a teacher, or insist that the head-teacher tells you or your parents what your rights are.

The school should tell you how long you are suspended for. Some don't, and this may be illegal. You should complain to the LEA if you are suspended indefinitely.

If you think the suspension was unreasonable, your parents can appeal to the Secretary of State for Education (see *Department of Education* above).

The LEA must make arrangements for you to be educated elsewhere while you are suspended, but there may be a long delay before another school or home tutor is found for you.

Pupils have been suspended for wearing jewellery to school, not wearing proper uniform, and so on, as well as for serious misbehaviour such as hitting a teacher or another pupil, refusing to work, or being absent for a long period without a good reason.

Transport

The LEA has to provide free transport to and from school if:
- you are under eight and the school is more than two miles away by the shortest possible route;
- you are eight or over and the school is more than three miles away.

The LEA is not entitled to refuse to pay your fares if the only route home which is under two miles involves a dangerous journey, e.g. walking through a wood.

The LEA can refuse to pay for your fare if there is a suitable school within that distance but your parents have chosen one further away.

The LEA can also, if it wants to, provide free travel for handicapped children or if they think it would be dangerous for you to walk home. If your parents have a low income, they can ask the LEA to pay your fares to school, even if you live within the two or three mile limit. If you think there is a special reason why you should get help with transport, it is always worthwhile getting your parents to ask the LEA.

'Truanting'

If you have never started at school, your parents can be compelled to send you there (see *Attendance*). Once you are enrolled at a school, your name is entered on the school register. The school has to inform the LEA if any of its registered pupils is not attending regularly or has been absent for more than two weeks without a medical certificate. You are not allowed to stay at home because someone else in your family is ill.

The LEA will then send an educational welfare officer to see you and your parents to try and get you to go to school. If the police pick you up while you're truanting, they can take you into police custody and refer you to the educational welfare officer.

If you still don't go to school, the LEA can take your parents to court for 'failing to secure your attendance'. Your parents will have to convince the court that:
- you were absent with the school's permission; *or*
- you were unable to go to school because you were ill or because some unavoidable reason prevented you from going.

If you were sent to school not wearing the proper uniform, and your parents knew you would be sent home for that reason, they can be convicted for failing to make sure you went to school.

Your parents can be fined up to £200. If they are convicted three or more times for failing to get you to go to school, they could in theory be sent to prison, although this doesn't happen in practice.

Fining or imprisoning parents isn't likely to be a very effective way of making you go to school. Some LEAs recognise that many pupils truant because they are bored at school, and have opened special truancy projects for young people who refuse to go to school. These projects have a small number of pupils and aim to give students more relevant work than their school-courses may do. If you persistently truant, you might be taken into care by the local council (see chapter 3).

26

Despite this legislation, which tends to blame young people for not attending school, the government hasn't made adequate educational provision for young travellers (people who live in mobile homes and travel from place to place), such as teachers to go to the travellers, and setting up a flexible structure to ensure that young travellers have continuity of education. Rather, it has decided that young travellers only have to receive half the education that other young people get.

Uniform

The LEA, the school governors and the head-teacher between them decide whether or not your school has a uniform. If it does, you will have to wear it. Your parents can apply to the LEA for a grant to help with the cost of the uniform (see *Money,* page 22).

If you don't obey the school rules on uniform, the school can send you home. If this happens repeatedly, your parents can be taken to court for failing to make sure that you go to school (see *Truanting*).

Rules on uniform can forbid you to wear jewellery. In one case, a girl who wore earrings in her pierced ears was refused entry by the school, and her parents were convicted for failing to send her to school. Boys may also be refused permission to grow beards, and girls may be banned from wearing trousers.

If you object to your school's rules on uniform, you should talk to the teachers and the head. Your parents could also take the matter up with the Parent-Teachers Association, the board of governors and the local council's education committee.

More Information

You can get more information, or help and advice, from the following organisations.

Advisory Centre for Education (ACE), 18 Victoria Park Square, London, E2 (01-980 4596). Can advise parents and pupils on education problems.

National Union of Students (01-272 8900). Advises on students' rights, grants, LEAs.

STOPP, 18 Victoria Park Square, London, E2 9PB (01-980 8523).

3
CHILDREN AND
YOUNG PEOPLE
IN CARE

If you are 'in care', the local authority will appoint a social worker to look after you. S/he will decide where you live, what school you go to, where you spend your holidays. Also s/he has a part in deciding how often you see your family, although both you and your family have a say in this as well.

You may be allowed to go on living at home even though you are in care, although if this happens the social worker is still responsible for you and can for example decide to remove you from home or make conditions regarding the way you live or are looked after. Alternatively, you may have to live in a community home, boarding school or with foster parents.

About 100,000 children are in care in this country. For every 1,000 people aged under 17, about seven are in care.

Why someone is put in care

Here are some examples of the things which may lead to your being taken into care:
– Your parents are dead or have abandoned you, and there is no relative to look after you properly.
– Your parents are ill or homeless and temporarily unable to look after you.
– You are being neglected or ill-treated at home, or in danger of this happening.
– You are under school-leaving age and persistently truanting and your parents can't or won't get you to go to school.
– You are in 'moral danger' (for girls under 16, this usually means sleeping around or being a prostitute; for boys, it usually means being at risk of homosexual contact. It also applies if you are sleeping rough, taking illegal drugs or thought to be mixing in 'bad company').
– You have been convicted of a criminal offence.

You won't necessarily be taken into care even if one or more of these things applies to you. We set out in detail below how children and young people can be taken into care (see pages 33-41).

A care order can be made on you until you reach the age of 18. Care orders usually end on your 18th birthday. But if you are taken into care at the age of

16 or 17, then the order sometimes lasts until you turn 19. No care order can be made if you are 16 or over and married.

Getting youself put in care

Some people are so desperate to leave home and get away from their parents that they actually try to get the council to take them into care. In fact, you have no right to insist on being taken into care. You can ask the local council's social services department, but they can only take care proceedings if one of the things mentioned by the law applies to you (these are described briefly above, and are set out in detail on pages 36-7). They cannot take you into care simply because you feel your parents are behaving unreasonably by not letting you go out in the evenings or at weekends. But if you are being battered, or sexually assaulted, or otherwise very badly treated at home, then you should certainly go to the social services department for help.

You have no legal right of access to social work files about you.

Where you will live if you're in care

You can't choose where you will live once you've been taken into care. This is one of the most important decisions which the local authority will take for you, and the social worker may not know where this will be until after you are in care. However, they are required to place you near your home, if possible, unless there is a special reason not to do so.

Each local authority has a register of approved foster parents, who are people willing to look after other people's children. The council has to approve foster parents before they can foster children in care. If the council fosters you with a family, the council will pay your foster parents an allowance for looking after you. The amount varies from authority to authority and usually goes up as you get older.

Community and voluntary homes

Community homes, which are usually paid for and run by local authorities, vary a great deal as they are designed to meet the needs of different children. Some are more secure, since they are designed to cope with children who would run away if they got the chance. Some have only younger children, others only have handicapped children, and so on.

There are government regulations on the way community homes are run and the facilities provided. The home must have adequate medical and dental facilities, and proper fire and safety precautions. The home must have facilities for family and friends to visit. You and your family, along with the home, have a say in how often you get visits. As far as practicable, the home must make arrangements for you to go to the religious services for your religion.

Young people who have reached the age of 16, but who are under 21, can go on living in a community home if they are working, training or studying nearby.

Voluntary homes, which are similar to community homes, are run and sometimes paid for by voluntary bodies, such as a charity or a church, or sometimes they are owned and run by ordinary families. Before a local council can send children to a voluntary home, they must inspect it to make sure it meets the required standards. The home then has to be regularly inspected to ensure that standards are kept up.

If you are living in a community or voluntary home, the local authority can insist that your parents pay something towards your upkeep. The amount they are asked to pay depends on their income, and in many cases parents are not asked to make any contribution. The amount involved cannot be more than the amount paid by the council to foster parents in its area. If the council and your parents can't agree on the sum they should pay, the council can ask the local magistrates' court to decide the amount and to make an order that they pay it.

The council can pay your parents' travelling expenses to visit you.

Secure Accommodation

Normally if you are in care the local authority cannot keep you in accommodation which restricts your liberty – you can't be kept somewhere

where you are locked up. However in certain circumstances the local authority may place you in such accommodation. They will normally do this if you keep on running away.

If you are under 10 years old you cannot be kept in secure accommodation unless the Secretary of State has given permission for this. If you are over 10 years old then the local authority can only keep you there for up to 72 hours. If they want to keep you on longer they must apply to the juvenile court for an order allowing them to do so. Notice of this hearing must be sent to you and your parents. You should get advice from a solicitor as soon as possible.

Before making an order, the court must be satisfied either that you have a history of absconding or are likely to abscond from any other sort of accommodation *and* that if you abscond it is likely that your physical, mental or moral welfare will be at risk, or that if you are kept in any other type of accommodation you are likely to injure yourself or others. There are special conditions for children remanded in care charged with criminal offences or convicted of offences where the punishment is 14 years or more for an adult (for example robbery, murder), and for children who have previously been convicted of an offence of violence. For those children, the local authority only has to satisfy the court that the child is likely to abscond or is likely to injure himself/herself or others if not kept in such accommodation.

Both you and your parent/s can be legally represented at the juvenile court hearing.

If the court is satisfied that the local authority have satisfied the conditions set out above, then it can make an order placing you in secure accommodation for up to 3 months. The court can make a further order but the total period must be 6 months or less. This does not stop the local authority applying again to the court for another order at the end of that time.

If you are placed in secure accommodation, the local authority must hold a review about your case every three months and must hear what you think. Some local authorities have decided to review cases on a monthly basis instead, which should give more protection to children.

Secure accommodation orders are very serious, as they take away your freedom and place you somewhere where you are locked up in much the same way as if you had been sentenced to a period in custody for committing a crime. You don't have to have committed a crime, however, to be made the subject of a secure accommodation order.

Even though you are in secure accommodation, you are entitled to continue to receive proper education and this point may need to be watched.

Your rights if you are in care

Young people don't have many rights under the present law, and this is even more true of young people in care. However, the local authority must act in your best interests and should, wherever possible, take account of your feelings before making decisions about you. They don't have to consult you if they think 'the interests of the public' demand otherwise (for instance, if you have been convicted of a serious crime).

The local authority has to review your case every six months. In practice such a review may not amount to very much. You should make your views clearly known to those attending the review and ask to be present if you feel that otherwise your views will not be taken into account properly. If those responsible for you refuse to let you go to the review, then you could write what you think and want on a piece of paper and insist that it be read out at the review. If you find this difficult then you could get a friend or friendly teacher to help.

If you are in a home, the people running it and your social worker will decide the rules about staying out in the evening or at weekends, how much pocket-money you get and so on. They also make the rules about punishments. Corporal punishment is still used in community homes, although it has to be 'reasonable'. Being locked up in solitary confinement is also used as a punishment, although you should not be locked up for more than 48 hours.

The local authority should bring you up in your own religion and does not have the right to change it. Generally your religion will be the one your parents have chosen for you although you may choose your own. There is no definite age at which the law considers you to be old enough to choose your own religion, although you clearly have the right to do so when you reach 18.

You can't be adopted while you are in care unless your parents agree, although it is possible for the court to do this without your parents' agreement if, for example, they think your parents are unreasonably refusing to agree. This could happen, for instance, if you have been with foster parents ever since you were very young and your natural parents have hardly kept in touch with you at all or your natural parents have been and are unable to look after you properly.

If you have to have medical treatment, the local authority has to consent on your behalf until you reach the age of 16. If you want to get married, you have to get them to agree to this until you reach the age of 18. If you want to emigrate, you need their agreement for this if you are under 18.

You can apply to be taken out of care. A solicitor can act on your behalf and can be paid from the legal aid fund. On page 41, we suggest some ways to get legal advice.

Your parents' rights and duties

When you are in care, your parents will normally have to contribute money towards the cost of maintaining you. (See above, page 30).

Your parents must tell the local authority their address, and any change of address, while you remain in care, but the local authority does not have to tell them where you are living.

When a care order is made to take you into care, your parents must *not* keep you at home without the consent of the local authority. If they disobey the care order, they are committing a criminal offence and could be prosecuted.

Your parents cannot withhold their consent to your having medical treatment or an operation, or getting married, if you are in care. It is up to the local authority, not your parents, to decide whether to agree. But your parents must be consulted if you want to emigrate.

Your parents can't force the local authority to bring you up in their own religion. But they can insist that you are not brought up in a religion which they disapprove of.

Seeing your parents and relatives while you are in care

The local authority has the power to decide where and how often you see your parents whilst you are in care, although they should discuss this with all concerned, you, your parent/s and your carers, and try to reach agreement about it.

There are government guidelines contained in a booklet called a Code of Practice which social workers should follow. If you are not seeing your parent/s, or other relatives, brothers and sisters, grandparents, aunts, uncles etc., as often as you would like, you can ask them to apply under the Code of Practice. Although the local authority cannot be made to allow your parent/s or relatives more 'access', there are arrangements for hearing about the difficulty at the highest level in the social services department, that is the Director of Social Services. And if s/he cannot settle matters to your parent/s' and relatives' satisfaction, then the councillors elected to your local authority should be brought in.

This whole question of contact between you and your relatives is looked on as an important one and the Code of Practice says the social worker has a definite responsibility to make sure contact takes place. It especially mentions people you may not have seen for a long time. And your parent/s should be invited to any case conferences where visiting is to be discussed.

If you do not want to see your parent/s it is unlikely you will be made to.

If you are stopped from seeing your parent/s

If the local authority decides to refuse to let your parent/s see you at all or fails to make any arrangements for them to do so, your parents, but not you, have the right to apply to the court for an access order. If the court grants this, it can lay down such conditions as it thinks right about the access your parent/s should have. At the court hearing you can be represented by a solicitor who can put your view, and the court can appoint a guardian *ad litem* to safeguard your interests in the same way as for the care case itself (see page 33). Your parent/s' solicitor may decide to have a report by a social worker unconnected with the authorities, an 'independent' social worker, who will help the solicitor make sure your parent/s' viewpoint is fully brought out before the court.

How you can be taken into care

In some cases, you may be taken into care 'voluntarily' – in other words, the council doesn't actually get an order placing you in care. Alternatively, the council can pass a 'parental rights resolution' or get a court order to take you into care. Or you may be taken into care because you have been convicted of a criminal offence. We will explain firstly when you can be taken into care 'voluntarily'. The ways in which courts can place you in care are dealt with on pages 36-8.

Voluntary care

Voluntary care does *not* mean that you volunteer to go into care. But if, for instance, your parents are ill they can ask the local council to take you into care until they are well enough to look after you again.

You can be taken into care without any care order being made if:
– you have no parent or guardian;
– you have, but they have abandoned you;
– you are lost;
– your parents or guardian are unable to look after you (e.g. because they are in prison)

You can only be taken into voluntary care if you are under 17. You can then be kept in care until your 18th birthday. But the council should try to get you back to your parents or a relative or other person capable of looking after you as soon as possible.

Your parents can take you away at any time – although if you have been in voluntary care for over six months, the local authority can make your parents give them 28 days' notice before taking you away. They can either write to the council saying they want you back, or they can just tell the social worker or the person running the home where you are living. It is better if they write as it avoids any misunderstanding.

Keeping you in care

If you are in voluntary care, the council may decide that it would be better for you to stay in care rather than go home – for instance, if you're in danger of being battered if you return home. They can keep you in care by passing a parental rights resolution which is a formal decision by the council to take over the legal responsibility for looking after you. You will then stay in care until you are 18 (unless the council decides to end the parental rights resolution), and you will go on living where your social worker decides. Your parents would only be able to get you back if the council agreed, or if they went to court and got the court's permission.

The council may decide to pass a parental rights resolution about you if:
– your parents are dead;
– they have abandoned you;
– they are unable to look after you, for instance because they are ill;
– they are considered unfit to look after you, perhaps because the local council thinks their way of life is unsuitable (for instance, if your mother is a prostitute);
– the council thinks your parents have consistently failed to carry out the usual duties of a parent (e.g. they haven't fed and clothed you properly);
– the council has already taken your brother or sister into care;
– you have been in voluntary care for three years.

Parental rights resolution

If a parental rights resolution is passed about you, the main difference for you is that you can no longer go and live at home again unless the council lets you, or a court agrees that your parents can have you back. You may not even know that the parental rights resolution is being passed until it's over.

The next section describes the legal formalities which are involved in a parental rights resolution.

If the social workers looking after you decide that the council should pass a parental rights resolution, they will probably hold a 'case conference' to discuss you, possibly inviting other people – for instance, a probation officer, educational welfare officer, police officer or doctor – who have been involved with you. Neither you nor your parents are likely to be invited to the case conference, although you and your parents may be told it's happening and asked what you think.

The social workers then report to the council's social services committee who can recommend to the full council that they pass a parental rights resolution on you. Again, it is very unlikely that you or your parents will be invited to the council meeting although things are changing and, following severe criticisms of this secret procedure, some councils do see the parents.

If the council passes the resolution then your parents will be sent a letter by the council saying that the resolution has been passed.

If your parents want to object to the parental rights resolution, they have to write to the council within one month, saying that they object. The parental rights resolution will then automatically end – unless the authority arrange for your case to be dealt with by the juvenile court. If they do this within 14 days of getting your parents' objections, then the resolution stays in force until the court has heard the case.

Most councils who have gone to the trouble of passing a parental rights resolution aren't going to let it drop just because your parents have objected. So what usually happens if your parents object is that the local juvenile court decides what should happen to you – and you stay in care until they decide.

At the juvenile court, your parents have the right to be represented by a lawyer and can apply for legal aid to cover the costs. The solicitor should get an independent social worker for the parents. The court can make you a party to the proceedings if it thinks it is necessary to do so to protect your interests. If the court does this it will usually also appoint a guardian *ad litem* to act on your behalf. The guardian *ad litem* will probably also instruct a solicitor to represent you. Both of these people are there to help you (see page 43 for more about how they work). Although no-one is accusing you or your parents of committing a crime, the actual procedure in the court is very similar to that in a criminal case (which is described on page 93).

After they have heard all the evidence, the magistrates have to decide whether the local authority had good reasons for passing the parental rights resolution when they did; whether those reasons still exist; and whether it is in your interest for you to stay in care. If they find all these conditions proved valid, then they can order that the parental rights resolution remains in force.

If the decision goes against them, your parents can appeal to the family division of the High Court. They will need a solicitor to organise this.

A parental rights resolution stays in force until you are 18. But your parents can apply to the court at any time to have it ended.

When the court orders you to be taken into care

The local authority can go to court because they think you ought to be in care. Or a juvenile court can decide to put you in care because you have been convicted of a criminal offence. But you may, of course, be allowed to go on living at home even after a care order has been made.

There are two main kinds of court orders:
– care orders
– place of safety orders

A juvenile court can make a care order if it is satisfied that you are not under the control of your parent or guardian.

Care Proceedings

You may be taken into care if one or more of the following conditions applies to you and if the juvenile court thinks that you will not get proper 'care and control' unless you are taken into care. Usually, the local council will apply to take you into care, but the National Society for the Prevention of Cruelty to Children (NSPCC), the police or the local education authority can also apply in certain circumstances.

You could be taken into care if the court is satisfied that any of the following things applies to you:
- Your proper development is being unnecessarily prevented or neglected.
- You are being ill-treated.
- The court has decided that another child living in your house (normally a brother or sister) is being neglected or ill-treated and they think you are likely to suffer in the same way.
- One of your parents, or a step-parent, or someone else living with you or coming to live with you has been convicted of a crime involving cruelty to children, and that, as a result, you are likely to be ill-treated or neglected.
- You are exposed to 'moral danger'. If you are a girl under 16 this means sleeping around or being a prostitute. Even if you are 16 or over, you can still be in 'moral danger' if you are sleeping around or mixing in what the court thinks is bad company. If you are a boy, 'moral danger' can mean being 'at risk' of homosexual contact. Taking illegal drugs, going to clubs late at night, living in a mixed flat or commune or sleeping rough could also lead the court to decide that you are in 'moral danger'. But you are less likely to end up in court if you can give the appearance of leading a respectable life – sharing accommodation with someone of the same sex, for instance – and if you can avoid your parents complaining to the police or the social services department. Things will be a lot more difficult for you if you are under school leaving age, since you probably won't have any money, and if you leave school to get a job this could be a reason for taking you into care.
- You are beyond the control of your parent or guardian, either because they are unable to control you or because you are uncontrollable.
- You are guilty of a crime. But if you are found guilty of murder or manslaughter, you cannot be put in care: you would be sent to prison or put in youth custody instead.
- You are not going to school regularly (this only applies if you are under school-leaving age).

If the court decides that one of these reasons applies to you, *and* that you are in need of 'care and control' which they feel you won't receive unless there is a court order, then one of the following orders will be made:
1. Your parents may be asked to promise to take proper care of you and exercise proper control over you, for up to three years (or until you turn 18). If they don't do this, they can be made to forefeit up to £200 to the court, and you could be taken into care by the council.
2. The court may pass a supervision order appointing a social worker to keep an eye on you for a certain period. You will probably still live at home.
3. The court may make a full care order. The social services department of the council takes over responsibility for you, as explained earlier on page 35. If you are under 16 when the care order was passed, it can last until you turn 18. If you are older than that when it is passed, it can last until you are 19.
4. The court can decide to send you to a mental hospital, or have a guardian appointed to take care of you. But this would only happen where they decided you were suffering from certain kinds of mental illness. It is very rare for the court to make such an order.

The next section explains the legal formalities in care proceedings. On page 41, we explain what to do if you (or your parents) want to get you out of care.

Before the court hearing

If the council wants to take you into care, it normally begins by informing the clerk of the local juvenile court what the grounds are for the care proceedings. The court should then send a copy of this notice to you, your parents and anyone with whom you have lived for more than six weeks in the last six months (usually your parents, but it could be your foster-parents, or a relative). If you are being taken into care because you have been accused of a criminal offence, and you are aged over 13, the local probation officer also has to be told.

After that, you and your parents should be sent a summons, telling you the time and the place where the case will be heard. In some cases, the council will want to take you away from your home before the case is heard: they can do that by applying for a place of safety order.

Place of safety orders

Probably the first thing you or your parents will know about a place of safety order is when the social worker (sometimes with police officers) arrives at your home to take you away.

A local authority social worker (or the police, the NSPCC or anyone concerned about your welfare) can apply for a place of safety order if s/he thinks you are being ill-treated or neglected, or in danger for any other reason. (This includes 'moral danger', as explained on page 37). Usually neither you nor your parents is told that this is happening and the local magistrate will make a place of safety order without hearing what you or your parents have to say. The magistrate should listen to the evidence of the social worker or official making the application, and should only make the order if s/he is satisfied that you are genuinely at risk. Orders are rarely refused.

Once a place of safety order has been made, you will usually be moved to a community home, a foster home or in some cases a hospital. It is an offence for your parents to refuse to obey the place of safety order. You have no right to appeal against the place of safety order, and nor have your parents. It can last for up to 28 days, by which time the local authority should have started legal proceedings or, if not, decided to return you home.

So once a place of safety order has been made, you just have to wait for it to run out. But you should use the time before the court meets to get yourself a lawyer, as explained in the next section.

How your interests will be looked after in care proceedings

Your parent/s

In care proceedings the court has to consider *your* interests and should decide what is best for you. Your parent/s, of course, should also be present in court and can express their views and give their side of the story.

The court starts by assuming that your parent/s can act on your behalf – this includes them instructing a solicitor for you. However, if the court considers that there is a conflict of interests between you and your parent/s, it must order that you be represented by someone else in court.

Your guardian ad litem

Once the court has made such an order it will appoint a *'guardian ad litem'*; which means a person who should represent your interests in care cases. The guardian ad litem is usually but not always a social worker who must not work for the local authority who is applying for a care order.

The guardian ad litem must make enquiries into all the circumstances which are relevant to your case. S/he must then prepare a report which will be given to the court.

Your solicitor

If a solicitor hasn't already been appointed and your guardian ad litem hasn't been told whether to appoint one or not, then s/he should ask the court whether a solicitor should be appointed to represent you. The court will probably tell the guardian ad litem to instruct a solicitor for you. In fact unless the court specifically says not, the guardian ad litem *must* instruct a solicitor. A solicitor should be instructed as soon as possible, so that his/her advice is available to you and your guardian ad litem from the beginning.

If you disagree with your guardian ad litem

Your guardian ad litem may not agree with your wishes. If s/he does not then you should insist that s/he makes your views known to the court. You also have the right to remain in court if you wish.

Better still, if it is clear to your solicitor that you don't go along with how the guardian ad litem sees things *and* your solicitor considers that you are old enough to know your own mind, then s/he no longer has to do what the guardian ad litem says and should act on your instructions.

Guardians ad litem must decide what they think will be in your interest and should try and obtain it, but if you disagree or feel dissatisfied, tell your solicitor, who will make sure the court is in no doubt as to your views.

An independent social worker

If you've disagreed with the guardian ad litem, s/he still goes ahead without legal representation and prepares a report. But where this has happened or if no guardian ad litem has been provided for you, your solicitor may consider having a report presenting your viewpoint prepared by a social worker who is separate from the social services department.

It's a lot of lawyers and social workers – but you may need them all to get what's best for you.

How to prepare yourself

It is often difficult for young people to say or know what they want in situations like this. If that is so then try and think carefully about what you want and say what that is. If that is impossible then try and discuss it with your guardian ad litem and/or your solicitor. Make it clear to them if necessary that you are unsure, and ask them what the consequences of the proceedings are if you don't know.

If you don't want what you say to be repeated to the court or anyone else, tell them so before you say it. Guardians ad litem don't operate under any rules which say what you tell them is confidential, so that if you are worried about this you should make it clear beforehand. Your solicitor should not repeat anything to the court that you have told him/her without your permission. So make the position clear first. Don't be afraid of your guardian ad litem or solicitor – they are there to help you get what's best for you.

Sometimes the court will appoint your solicitor first and your guardian ad litem later. Then the same rules apply as before.

Interim care orders

When the case comes to court, you may find that the court is not ready to deal with it – perhaps because the social workers haven't had time to talk to you and your parents and prepare a report or because the guardian ad litem hasn't prepared his/her report. If this happens, the court can put off the case (it's called an adjournment) and make a temporary care order, putting you in care of the local council until the case can be heard. The temporary order is called an *interim care order,* and cannot last for more than 28 days. The court can go on making new interim care orders until the case is heard – so that you could be taken into care temporarily for months on end.

You or your lawyer can object to an interim care order being made. If it is made anyway, you can appeal to the Crown Court. You can also apply to the High Court to have the order overturned. Your lawyer should explain these possibilities, and take the necessary steps.

If you are taken into care under a temporary order, you may still be allowed to live at home. But if the council thinks it is urgent to get you away from your home (for instance, if they believe you are at risk of being beaten), they may insist that you go and live in a community home.

At the court

On the day when the case is due to be heard, you and your parents and your lawyer will have to turn up at the court. This will be the local juvenile court and the people who will deal with your case are local magistrates. You should usually be there unless, of course, you are ill, although the court can order that a child under five doesn't have to come. If the court thinks that you may be upset by hearing all the evidence, or that this would be unsuitable for you to listen to, they will probably talk to you at the beginning of the case and then ask you to leave.

If you want to stay, then you can insist on doing so. This is something you and your solicitor ought to talk about beforehand. There are advantages and disadvantages in staying in court. The advantages are that you know what is being said and can alert your solicitor if people are not giving a true account of what has happened or of what you have said. The disadvantages are that it can be very upsetting indeed for you and your parents.

At the beginning of the case, the magistrate should explain to you or your parents why the care order has been applied for and what the case is about. After that, people speak and witnesses are called, in much the same order as in a criminal case – even though care proceedings are *not* criminal cases. (In chapter 9, we set out in detail the order in which things happen in a criminal case.)

If the council wants to take you into care because they say your parents aren't looking after you properly, your parents should be given a chance to question the council's representatives or any witnesses the council calls. Your parents can also call their own witnesses, or speak to the court themselves, to explain why they think they are looking after you properly. Your solicitor also has the right to call witnesses and you yourself can give evidence if you wish.

If, after listening to all the evidence, the magistrates decide that the local authority is right, they can also look at written reports prepared by social workers, probation officers or your school. They will also consider the report prepared by your guardian ad litem at this stage.

At the end of all this, the court decides whether to get your parents to promise to look after you properly, or whether to make a supervision order or a care order. These were explained on page 37.

Other ways the court can order you to be taken into care

In addition to the legal procedures outlined above, the local council can apply to have you made a ward of court. (See page 13 for more on this).

In any legal dispute about who should look after you or have custody of you the court may also decide that it would be better for a care order to be made. Finally, the court could order the local council to take you into care if you are convicted for a criminal offence.

Getting out of care

Once a care order has been made, it stays in force until you are 18. (If you were 16 or 17 when it was made, it stays in force until you are 19 unless you are adopted.)

If you wish, you can appeal against the care order immediately after it is made. You have to do this within 21 days and the appeal goes to the Crown Court (which has a judge who is more senior than the magistrates who heard the first case). You should talk to a lawyer about an appeal immediately after the care order is made.

Once you have been taken into care, you or your parents can apply at ·.ny time to the juvenile court to have the care order ended. If you fail the first time, you have to wait at least three months before applying again. You should contact a local law centre or Citizens' Advice Bureau to get a lawyer to help you if you want to have your care order ended. You can of course if you wish go back to the solicitor you had for the proceedings when the care order was made.

A guardian ad litem and a solicitor will usually be appointed to act for you in the same way as when the original care proceedings were brought.

If your parents have applied to take you out of care, and you don't want to go back to them, you should tell the social worker, the guardian ad litem, your lawyer and if necessary the court exactly how you feel about it. You should be given, and if you are not you should demand, the opportunity to speak to your guardian ad litem, solicitor, parents or social worker alone.

If the court decides to end the court care order, they may substitute a supervision order – which means that you live at home under your parents' care, but a social worker is appointed to keep an eye on you and them. Or they may simply end the care order without putting anything in its place.

It is often difficult for people who leave care at the age of 18 to find a place of their own to live. Social workers can help you buy the things you need (e.g. cooking things for your bedsitter or flat) by getting money from the local council, and some councils provide accommodation for children leaving care either in special flats or in ordinary council flats. It is worth asking your social worker if this is possible.

Further information

Children's Legal Centre 20 Compton Terrace, London N1 2UN. Tel: 01-359 6251

Voice for the Child in Care c/o 60 Carysfort Road, London N8 8RB (01-348 2588). A support group for children and young people in care.

National Association of Young People in Care (NAYPIC) Rooms 21-22, The Wool Exchange, Market Street, Bradford BD1 1LD (0274-72884), and 20 Compton Terrace, London N1 2UN (01-226 7102).

Black and In Care 20 Compton Terrace, London N1 2UN (01-226 7102).

4
EMPLOYMENT, UNEMPLOYMENT AND JOB TRAINING

The law on what age you have to be before you can do various jobs is complicated, and its effect varies from area to area. Broadly speaking, the rules are as follows:

If you are under 13, it is illegal for you to work unless you have an entertainment licence (this is explained below).

If you are aged 13, 14 or 15, you can take a part-time job, for not more than two hours on any school day. You can't work during school hours (9am to 4.30pm including the lunch hour). You can't start work before 7am or go on after 7pm.

The dinner break is part of the school day and you cannot use it to work in

On Saturdays, you can work for eight hours, but only for two hours on Sundays.

But your local authority can make regulations which apply locally and which may be stricter than these general rules. You can get a copy from the town hall.

The local authority can stop you doing any job at all if it thinks that the work will interfere with your education or welfare. If it thinks the job will damage your health or education, it can serve a notice on your employers forbidding them to employ you or imposing conditions on your employment.

You can only do 'light work', so you are not meant to do work involving heavy lifting. You cannot engage in street trading.

Whilst you are of compulsory school age, i.e. under 16, you are banned from working in manufacturing, demolition, mining, building, transport industries, or a sea-going ship or fishing boat unless the boat is one in which only your family is employed. Most local authorities have local rules banning you from working in kitchens, cake shops, restaurants, slaughterhouses, billiard saloons, gaming or betting shops or any business requiring door-to-door selling or touting although you should see the later section on work experience.

No-one under 18 is allowed to be employed in a bar.

These rules are very frequently broken. Someone who employs you in breach of the law can be prosecuted and, if s/he is convicted, fined. But this happens very rarely. *You* would not be breaking the law.

If you are aged 16 or over and have left school, you are free to work under the same conditions as adults. (There are, however, laws limiting the hours young people can work, for example, in mines). But if you stay on at school after 16, the Local Education Authority (LEA) can impose conditions on you remaining at school – for instance, making it a rule that you mustn't have a part-time job.

Markets and street trading

In general, you are not allowed to work on a market stall or become a street trader until you are 17. But some local authorities let you work on your parents' stall once you reach the age of 14. Ask at the town hall for details. Again, this rule is often broken and rarely enforced.

Entertainment

You cannot usually have time off school to take part in plays, films, TV shows or other entertainments unless you have a licence from the local authority. You will only get a licence if the LEA is satisfied about the arrangements made for your education and welfare. The licence will specify the times you can be absent from school.

You can get more information on this from a book called *The law on performances by children* published by Her Majesty's Stationery Office (write to HMSO, High Holborn, London WC1).

You don't need a licence to perform in things like the school play or the occasional charity performance.

Earnings

Any money you earn is legally yours, not your parents. Although you can be taxed, the number of hours you can work is so restricted you are unlikely to earn enough for this to happen. The wages paid to school-children are notoriously low, and many employers will use you as cheap labour.

Conditions at work

The conditions under which people work are controlled by law. All offices, shops and factories must have a certain number of toilets; premises must be kept clean; there must be proper fire precautions; and the building must be safe. There should be a notice on display setting out the regulations.

At the age of 16, you can join a trade union. Unions provide valuable benefits for their members, particularly by negotiating better wages and conditions. If you are sacked or victimised, your union should fight the case. If you are injured at work, the union can advise you on getting compensation, and many unions provide sick pay for their members. Find out who is the shop steward or union representative at your place of work. If you're not sure which union to join, contact the Trades Union Congress, Great Russell Street, London WC1, who will tell you.

When you start work for more than 16 hours a week, you should get a statement of the terms and conditions of employment, telling you what your pay is, whether you will get sick pay or holiday pay, and so on. If you don't get this statement, ask for it.

Detailed information about workers' rights and the law is contained in *Your Rights at Work* (published by NCCL).

The Armed Forces

You can join the armed forces at the age of 16 if you are male, or 17 if you are female. But you need your parents' agreement until you are 18. If you join before you are 17½ (males) or 18 (females), you can leave within the first 6 months by giving 14 days' notice. You don't have to pay anything to leave.

Men who join between 17½ and 18 can leave within the first six months, or before they reach the age of 18 years and 3 months. They have to forfeit 7 days' gross pay – except in the case of juniors, apprentices and young soldiers, sailors and airmen in which case there is no penalty. After that, it gets much more difficult to leave the armed forces.

Getting a job

The careers teacher at your school or college should discuss with you the various kinds of work available and help you decide what to do. S/he should also know about the different training schemes.

You should make up your own mind about what work you want to do, and while most careers teachers will try to find a job that suits you, a few will try and make up your mind for you. This is particularly true for girls who are often pushed into so-called 'women's jobs' such as clerical or shop work. But sex discrimination is now unlawful and if you want to do a job that is traditionally thought of as 'men's work' (or if you are a boy and you want to do an untraditional job such as secretarial work), you should not let yourself be pressured into something else.

The careers teacher should be able to help arrange interviews with prospective employers.

If there is no careers teacher or adviser at your school or college, you should contact the careers officer for your area (look in the phone book under the local education authority).

Job Centres

As well as looking in local papers for jobs, you can visit the local Job Centre (look in the phone book). Job Centres, which are run by the government, have a large number of jobs displayed on cards. You just pick the card which interests you, take it to the receptionist who will fix an interview for you. But a Job Centre cannot give you detailed advice or help about which job is suitable for you.

The Careers Officer will be able to advise you on the different jobs available.

Work Experience

Many schools take part in work experience programmes where in your last year at school you can spend some part of the time training for a job, e.g. by working in a garage. In this case, some of the restrictions placed on young people working will not apply. If you are interested in such a scheme you should ask about it at school.

Apprenticeships and day-release

Many employers offer apprenticeships or time off during work to allow you to attend college. The careers officer should be able to give you information about these. The Sex Discrimination Act states that apprenticeships must be open to both boys and girls. Although far fewer girls than boys get apprenticeships, and most girls' apprenticeships are in hairdressing, there is nothing to stop you going for an apprenticeship for much better-paid work, for instance as a printer, engineer or builder.

46

Some employers provide good on-the-job training, such as the civil service and local government. But you should ask any employer where you go for an interview about what training opportunities they provide.

The *Personnel and Training Data Book,* published by Kogan Page, lists industrial training courses. Get this at the local library.

Going to college

Many jobs require you to have GCEs or CSEs or other exams before they will employ you. If you didn't do them at school, you can do them later. Colleges of further education provide full and part-time courses, and you may actually prefer studying for the exams in a college where you are treated as an adult, rather than at school. The careers office can tell you about the courses available locally.

Further Education Colleges also provide a wide range of vocational courses (that is, courses qualifying you for a particular kind of job) on a full – or part-time basis. Again, the careers office can give you information.

Studying for a degree

You can apply for a place at university or polytechnic when you are 17, although you can't actually enrol until you are 18. You should ask your teachers about the different courses available. You could also look at the *Directory of Degree Courses,* which should be at your local library. Another useful publication is *How to apply for admission to a university* (from UCCA, Rodney House, Rodney Road, Cheltenham, Gloucestershire).

The Higher Education Advisory Centre, 114 Chase Side, Southgate, London N14 (01-886 6599) provides information on higher education courses and grants.

Grants

The LEA for your area must give you a grant to do a:-
– first degree course;
– course recognised as equivalent to a degree course;
– Higher National Diploma Course;
– teacher training course;
– course leading to a diploma in Higher Education.

You may be refused a grant if you haven't been resident in the United Kingdom for the three years leading up to 1 September in the year when your course starts. But you will still get the grant if your parents or husband or wife were employed outside the UK during that time.

You may also be refused a grant if the LEA thinks your behaviour makes you 'unfit' to get a grant, or if you have already attended a course for which you got a grant, or if you are under 25 and have already attended two years' full-time further education outside the UK.

The amount of grant depends on the resources of your parents or your husband or wife. The National Union of Students (address below) negotiates the level of grant with the Department of Education. The grant is meant to cover your fees and living expenses.

In addition, the LEA can award a grant for a course other than those listed above, or may give a grant to a student who wouldn't normally qualify. It is always worth trying. The NUS can advise you on the attitude of your particular LEA, and can advise on charities and trusts which may be able to help if your LEA won't.

Maternity benefits

If you're going to have a baby, you can claim a *maternity grant*. This is a tax-free, lump sum of £25 to help with immediate costs. Get form BM4 from your ante-natal clinic. From April 1987 the Maternity Grant will be means-tested and only available to women on the lowest incomes.

Maternity allowance: You can get a weekly allowance of £29.45 for 18 weeks, starting 11 weeks before the birth. You can only claim if you have fulfilled certain National Insurance contributions. After 1987, it will depend on your previous *work* record rather than National Insurance contributions. This means fewer women will be eligible to claim.

If you are having a baby and are not married, you should claim supplementary benefit for the period when you don't work. If you're married and living with your husband, you can't claim supplementary benefit: only the man can claim and, of course, if he's earning he can't claim benefit!

If you're reading this after April 1987, the Social Security Act will change your maternity rights. Check with your local security office, Citizens Advice Bureau or the Maternity Alliance. (See *Maternity Rights at Work* (NCCL) by Jean Coussins, Lyn Durward and Ruth Evans.)

If you are unemployed

Most unemployed people who are signing on have to apply for supplementary benefit. You only receive unemployment benefit, which is different, if you were working the previous year and paid National Insurance contributions. Anyway, many people find that their unemployment benefit is not enough and have to apply for supplementary benefit as well. N.B. The Social Security Act 1986 is radically changing the system. If you're reading this after April 1987, check with your social security office, or phone the DHSS Freefone by dialling 100 and asking the operator for it, or contact the Child Poverty Action Group's Advice Line (01-405 5942).

Supplementary benefit

Supplementary benefit is a 'means tested' benefit. This means that you'll have to answer a lot of questions about your situation. According to your answers, the DHSS (Department of Health and Social Security) will decide how much someone in your position should get.

However, you are able to get a basic rate, although this varies according to your age and whether you are living at home, or independently in your own accommodation, or with someone else. In 1986 these 'weekly scale rates' were: person living independently £29.80 (long-term, £37.90); couple £48.40 (long-term £60.65); person living at home, age 16-17 £18.40; person living at home, age 18+ £23.85. In addition to this you might be able to get money for extra heating, a special diet, outstanding Hire Purchase payments, or if you're blind. You need to check these with your local social security office (or DHSS Freefone) after April 1987. If you're getting any National Insurance benefits (i.e. unemployment benefit), any earnings over £4 after tax and work expenses will be *subtracted* from what you would otherwise get. This means that the more money you get from other sources, the less you will receive as supplementary benefit. You can have some savings, but if you have over £3,000 you won't be entitled to supplementary benefit. If you own a house, its value doesn't count against you.

For young people with a disability

You may be entitled to an attendance allowance – this is payable to *you*, although before you are 16 it is normally paid to your parent or foster parent. It is meant to help you get the care you need as a person with a disability, and you can spend it as you wish. You might also be able to get Severe Disablement Allowance when you are 16. You can apply for SDA whilst you are receiving education or further education, if your course is geared to people with disabilities. Neither of these allowances affect how much supplementary benefit you are entitled to.

Studying at college

If you are unemployed, you can study at college for up to 12 hours a week without this affecting your supplementary benefit. You can study full-time non-advanced further education for up to 21 hours *as long as you have been signing on for 3 months before the course starts*. If you are a full-time student, you will only be entitled to supplementary benefit during the summer vacation. Students who are living in college accommodation will not be able to claim Housing Benefit while getting a grant (from the beginning of the Autumn Term to the end of the Summer Term). Housing Benefit is available to all students *only* during the summer vacation. If you are paying a high rent (in *non-college* accommodation) you may be eligible for housing benefit during term time. There is an amount in the student grant (£13.60 outside London, £17.70 in London in 1986) which is supposed to cover accommodation costs. If in doubt, contact the National Union of Students (01-272 8900).

For women

Women often have difficulty in claiming supplementary benefit for themselves. If you are married, or the DHSS decides you are living with someone as a 'couple', then you can't usually claim supplementary benefit in your own right. The man claims for you and, of course, if he is earning he won't get benefit. However, if you are both unemployed, you can claim for both of you, if you have been employed during the last six months.

If you want to argue against the DHSS's definition of you as part of a 'couple', you can do so by telling them that you don't sleep together and/or there is a strict division of living costs, for example, you pay exactly half of the bills and you buy your own food.

If you are a young mother under 16 you won't be able to claim supplementary benefit. However, you can get child benefit – £7.10 in 1986. If you are bringing up a child or children on your own you can also get the

Single Parent Addition – £4.60 in 1986. You are also eligible for an automatic maternity grant of £25 (although this is changing in April 1987 and will be 'means-tested' from then on). you can claim this from the 26th week of pregnancy up to 3 months after the birth, although the payment won't be made until 3 weeks before the baby is due. You are also entitled to: free prescriptions and dental care whilst you are pregnant and for 1 year after the baby is born; and single payments for baby things and maternity clothes for yourself. If you are 16 or over you can claim benefit in your own right. You will be able to claim when you leave school or when the baby is born whichever comes first.

If you were working and paid enough National Insurance contributions in the previous years, then you will also be entitled to Maternity Allowance – this lasts for several weeks before and after the baby is born. After April 1987, this will become the Statutory Maternity Allowance and will be calculated on your previous work record.

Mothers under 16 are unlikely to be able to get Maternity Allowance and can't get supplementary benefit, even though they need the money just as much as other mothers, if not more.

Extra money for everyone

To qualify for Single Payments you must need a particular item and have nothing that will do in its place. The sort of items for which you can get a single payment include: household expenses such as floor covering, light fittings, a cooker, etc; clothing and footwear where the need doesn't arise from normal wear and tear; special expenses such as removal expenses, draught proofing or reasonable legal fees. From April 1987, single payments are to be abolished and replaced by a new Social Fund (under the Social Security Act 1986). You may be able to get a grant *or a loan:* it will be at the discretion of your local social security office.

How to claim

If you are a school leaver aged 16 or 17 you have to wait until the first of the following dates after you left school: the first Monday in January, the Monday after Easter Monday, or the first Monday in September. You then make your claim. You have first to register for work at the local careers office; they will give you a card to take to the unemployment benefit office. If you are 19 or over, you can claim as soon as you leave school by going straight to the unemployment benefit office.

Form B1 is dealt with by the DHSS, and unless you are getting any of the National Insurance benefits, your only future contact with the Department of (un) Employment will be once a week/fortnight/month when you sign on as unemployed and available for work. Consequently, if you have any difficulty in completing the B1 form or at a later stage in your claim for supplementary benefit, you should ask for an interview with the DHSS, which will be in a different building from that of your local unemployment benefit office.

The B1 form asks many questions concerning your personal relationships and living arrangements. From the answers you give, the DHSS assesses how much money someone in your situation needs to live, and how much

50

you are already receiving. Your allowance will be paid by Girocheque fortnightly provided you sign it regularly at the times laid down.

You should be given form A14N which gives a very limited explanation of how your allowance has been worked out. If you want a *full* explanation then you should ask for form A124. This is a large form with 4 sides to it, don't accept anything less!

Difficulties in getting what you are entitled to?

If there are any mistakes on forms A14N and A124 or if you are unhappy with how your allowance has been worked out, you can ask for it to be revised; or, if it looks as if the DHSS is dragging its feet, you can put in a written claim for an *urgent needs payment* and/or you can appeal.

If one of your girocheques doesn't arrive, inform the DHSS and the local unemployment benefit office. You'll probably have to go into the DHSS to make a written statement about the circumstances in which the giro went missing – take a friend with you! You probably won't get your money for a long time – so while you're in the DHSS, put in a claim in writing for an *urgent needs payment*. Make sure you sign the claim. Don't be put off in the DHSS; it is the duty of the supplementary benefit staff there to take a claim in writing from you.

If you are refused an urgent needs payment you can appeal against this decision.

Offers you cannot refuse?

Pressure on claimants is twofold; offers of employment or training which are often short term, menial and/or badly paid, coupled with the insinuation that you aren't entitled to any money. This pressure will probably start as soon as you leave school.

If you are a school leaver aged 16 or 17 you will be offered a place in the Youth Training Scheme (YTS) for which you get an allowance of £27.30 (£35.00 for the second year) a week. If you unreasonably refuse such a place or you leave the scheme before it is finished, your SB may be reduced by 40% for six weeks. If this happens you should consider making an appeal.

You might be called in for an interview with the Unemployment Review Officer (URO) whose job is to check up on unemployed claimants. If you don't attend this interview, your SB will be cut off. It's a good idea to keep all details of jobs you've applied for or been interested in and you should take these with you if you have such an interview. You can take along a friend for support when you go to the interview. You don't have to accept any unsuitable work you are offered, but take down any details of such work that the URO might offer you so that you can go and get support from your local trades council, if the URO stops, reduces or withholds your benefit you can appeal immediately.

You might also come into contact with the Specialist Claims Control Unit (SCCU). People from there go round different areas 'investigating' claimants. If they pick on you they will check your records, ask your neighbours questions and may even liaise with the police. You might then be called in for an interview, where the SCCU might well try to get you to withdraw your claim. The SCCU are not empowered to make any decisions about your entitlement to benefit, so if you can get support and advice from your local Claimant's Union or the Child Poverty Action Group (CPAG), you will be able to stand up to them.

How to appeal

You can appeal against almost any decision or refusal which leaves you dissatisfied. But you normally only have 4 weeks in which to submit the appeal from the time that the DHSS made their decision.

If the appeal cannot be held immediately, or if you are in urgent need of money, then the local SB office should pay you an urgent needs payment up to the day of the appeal hearing. Electricity and gas disconnections can be postponed if you write to the fuel boards concerned and tell them you have submitted an appeal and are awaiting the outcome of the hearing. Appeals can sometimes be heard at very short notice if there is an urgent reason.

To appeal you should write a letter stating the DHSS decision which you are unhappy about. The letter should be signed and dated – and keep a copy of it in case the DHSS 'lose' it.

To prepare your appeal you should make sure that any material evidence and/or witnesses are available for the hearing. Make sure you have a 'representative' for the hearing. You can get an hour's free legal advice from any legal aid solicitor; and you can also get help from your nearest Claimants' Union or Law Centre.

Important: Your right to appeal will be changed under the Social Security Act 1986. There is *no* right of appeal against decisions made by the new Social Fund. If you're not sure of your rights, contact the Child Poverty Action Group and the Claimants' Union to get advice.

Housing Benefit

Housing benefit is money to pay your rent and rates – it is administered by your local council. If you are on a low wage or if you aren't getting enough money from your unemployment and child benefits, then you should go and ask for an application form from your local council. If you are on supplementary benefit, the DHSS will send a form to your local council telling them to deal with your rent and rates.

If you live in private rented accommodation, the council will send you the money to pay your landlord. If you are a council tenant you won't get any money paid direct to you, but the council will arrange it so that you don't have to pay them any money for rent and rates either.

When you are living on little money, it is often difficult to pay for several things at once, for example, you may not have enough money to buy new clothes *and* pay your rent for that week. If you are living in private housing you have the money 'in your hand', so you can always buy the new clothes and put off paying the rent for a week. But if you are living in council housing, you don't have that choice – after paying for food and bills you may never have enough money in hand to buy new clothes. Do you think that because you live in council housing you should be denied the right to organise your own finances?

Living in lodgings or bed and breakfast

The new Supplementary Benefit regulations mean that if you are under 26 and are signing on and living in lodgings or bed-and-breakfast, you'll only get the money from the DHSS to pay the full cost of your accommodation for a very short period of time at the beginning of your stay in lodgings. This 'initial period' is 8 weeks in Birmingham, Glasgow, London and Manchester; 2 weeks in most coastal areas; and 4 weeks elsewhere. After that you won't be entitled to board and lodging allowance again until 6 months have passed since you moved into the lodgings. Even after 6 months you just get money for another 'initial period' before it is stopped again. When your board and lodging allowance stops coming through, you can move to a different area and make a fresh claim for board and lodging – but you have to keep moving every few weeks to keep making fresh claims.

If you get ill, the initial period will be extended by the same amount of time that you are ill. If the person making the claim gets a job, then the initial period will be extended by the length of time in work, but at least for 15 days. If the job ends in under 6 months and you didn't use up all of your initial period before you got the job, then you'll get an allowance for what was left over. If the job lasts for more than 6 months, then the new regulations don't apply as long as you remain at the same address.

The new regulations also don't apply if you:
– have a child or are pregnant
– are very sick, have a mental or physical disability, or are suffering from a mental disorder.
– have been in the accommodation for 6 months and were getting supplementary benefit without signing on
– are a student living in your usual term-time accommodation and you are applying for supplementary benefit during the summer vacation
– have been in local authority care in the last year
– have gone into board and lodgings because it was recommended for you by a government department, health authority, local authority, voluntary organisation, or the probation and afer-care service.
– are aged 16-18 and a) don't have anyone who is a parent to you; b) have left your family because you were in 'physical or moral danger'; c) are in local authority care but have to pay for your accommodation to someone else.

5
MONEY AND PROPERTY

You are entitled to own money regardless of your age and if your parents are given money for you then they must normally hold it for you on your behalf. Anyone of any age can open a bank account, either a deposit account (where you earn interest on the money you keep in the bank) or a current account (where you have a cheque book but where most banks do not give you any interest). You may find, however, that banks are reluctant to let people who have not yet left school, and who therefore have no earnings, have a current account. This is because if you 'overdraw' (write cheques for more money than you have in the account) they may not be able to get it back from you.

Special rules apply to the National Savings Bank. You cannot deposit unless someone over that age does it for you. You can deposit money in a Trustee Savings Bank at any age but if you are under seven you cannot Trustees Savings Bank at any age but if you are under seven you cannot withdraw it. If you are under seven and have money in either the National Savings Bank or a Trustee Savings Bank and it is proved to the bank that money is urgently needed for your maintenance, education or benefit or there are other reasons, then the bank can pay sums from the account to anyone who satisfies them that s/he will use the money for your benefit. Apart from these restrictions you can draw your money out as and when you wish.

Pocket money
There is no law that says that your parents or guardian have to give you pocket money.

Income tax
If you earn money then you have to pay income tax if your total earnings are more than the minimum level at which tax has to be paid. This figure is changed annually. From April 1985 the maximum you can earn in any year before paying tax was £2205. This is likely to be increased each April. In most jobs the tax is deducted from your wages before you get paid. This is called PAYE (Pay As You Earn). So if you haven't worked for a whole year, and you think you are paying too much tax, ask your employer for the address of your tax office and get them to check it for you. Also you can apply for a tax rebate (your money back) if you've been paying tax on your job but haven't earned enough (£2205 at the moment) to be taxed.

Until you are aged 18 your father (or your mother if she has custody of you) should make a tax return for you on his or her income tax form. If your earnings have been taxed on the PAYE system then this is not a problem, but if you have not been taxed then s/he will have to pay. Then s/he is entitled to keep money out of your earnings to pay this tax.

Of course many small employers who employ young people pay them out of petty cash or till receipts so that they don't have to account for the money. Then no one knows that you have earned the money and so you don't get taxed on it. This is not legal and if the Inland Revenue find out they can demand the tax due and can prosecute you and your employer.

Contracts

In law, a contract is an agreement between at least two people. This means that just buying an article from someone means that you have actually entered into a contract with them. So obviously you enter into contracts well before you reach the age of 18.

Although you can enter into contracts before you are 18, the law treats you differently from adults in that in general you are not bound by the agreement even though the other party to it is. There are three main exceptions to this. The first arises where the contract is for the purchase of goods or services which are essential for you such as food, clothing, medicine, or somewhere to live. The law calls such goods 'necessaries'. The other two sorts of binding contracts are contracts for apprenticeships and contracts of employment.

In these three cases you are legally bound by the contract and can be sued if you break it. In other cases if you have acted fraudulently in breaking the contract you may be bound by it in law.

None of this stops you being a partner in a firm or a member of a company, building society or industrial provident society. If you are a partner in a firm, however, unlike adults, you are not liable for the firm's debts or the acts of your partners. Partnership assets can be used to pay off partnership debts before you get your share.

Liability for other acts committed by you

You can be liable in law for certain types of behaviour if harm has resulted to others. Examples of this are trespassing on other people's property and causing damage, damage done by your pets, taking other people's property and selling it, damaging or refusing to return it.

You can only be liable for such acts if you are of such an age as to be able to distinguish between right and wrong. In certain circumstances your parents can be liable, for instance where they could have stopped you or if they allowed you to do the damage.

Borrowing money

There is nothing in law to stop you borrowing money at any age, but since in most cases the person who lends it to you will not be able to sue you for it if you can't repay it, you might well find it difficult to find someone prepared to lend it to you.

Property

While you are under eighteen years old you cannot own land or what the law calls real property. This includes houses, buildings of whatever kind and land regardless of what it is used for. This only applies to property in this country and different rules may apply to property situated abroad. If you inherit or otherwise acquire real property whilst you are under eighteen then it will be looked after for you by other people, known as trustees, until you are eighteen. Usually if you inherit property it will be under someone's will which provides the names or details of the trustees to look after it for you. If there is no will then the law still says that the property must be held in trust and a court can if necessary appoint trustees to look after it for you. Trustees have a duty to act in your interests and to manage the property properly. If they don't they can be penalised by the court.

6
SEX, RELATIONSHIPS AND MARRIAGE

This chapter is specifically about how the law treats sexual relationships and marriage. On page 66 we suggest a number of organisations which can give you more help and advice if you're having a hard time.

When a girl and a boy have an unlawful sexual relationship, it is the boy and not the girl who can be punished under the criminal law (except when the girl is 16 or over and the boy is not). This is because the law treats women as property and men as the possessors of that property – women as the things that men want, as if women didn't have desires of their own. The age of consent, 16, applies to women, but there is no age of consent for men as far as heterosexual sex is concerned. This age of consent was set in 1885 and it enabled the men who made the law and set the standards for society to retain control over the bodies of young women.

The law is also prejudiced against homosexual relationships – the age of consent for young men is 21, and the law doesn't recognise lesbian relationships at all so there is no age of consent as such.

In addition to the age of consent it is possible for young women and young men to be taken into care on the grounds of 'moral danger'. 'Moral danger' is a phrase used to cover a wide area of relationships which adults (particularly adult men) feel threatened by. 'Moral danger' doesn't necessarily have anything to do with what the young people concerned think – it can apply to: a young man who *is thought to be* having a homosexual relationship; a young woman who is having a lesbian relationship or sleeping with her boyfriend or who *is thought to be* 'promiscuous'.

But the law is much tougher in theory than in practice.

Sex between males and females
It is illegal for a boy or man to have sexual intercourse, or any other kind of sexual intimacy with a girl who is under 16; this is known as the age of consent. But a girl cannot be prosecuted for unlawful sexual intercourse if she has sex with boys of any age. She *could,* however, be prosecuted for indecent assault if the boy is under 16.

Girls and women in heterosexual relationships
You cannot be prosecuted for having sex at any age. (The only exceptions are incest, which is explained on page 65, and indecent assault on a boy aged under 16 – but prosecutions are extremely rare.)

Usually, the law will not interfere if you and your boyfriend decide to have a sexual relationship before you are 16. But if your parents object, or if you have left home, it is possible that the local authority might decide to take you into care on the grounds that you are in 'moral danger'. This can happen if the social workers think you are sleeping with your boyfriend or are likely to, or if they think you are promiscuous or at risk of becoming involved in prostitution. You can be taken into care on 'moral danger' grounds even after you have reached the age of 16, when it is legal for your boyfriend to have sex with you.

Chapter 3 gives more information on being taken into care.

For advice on contraception, see pages 61-2. We also list, on page 65, other books you can read about sexual relationships and places you can go to for help and advice.

Boys and men in heterosexual relationships

If you are under 14, you cannot be charged with 'unlawful sexual intercourse' for having sex with a girl who is under age. You could be charged with 'indecent assault' even if she consents, although this charge is rarely brought. Also you can't be prosecuted for rape, although you could be charged with indecent assault or attempted rape if you attack a girl or woman. (More about the law on assault and rape on page 64).

If you are aged 14 or over, and have sex with your girlfriend before she reaches 16, you can be charged with 'unlawful sexual intercourse'. You could be fined, sent to borstal, attendance centre or detention centre if you are convicted. If the girl was aged 13 or over, and you haven't been charged with the same offence before, you can defend yourself if you had reason to believe that the girl was actually aged 16 or over. In practice, there are very few prosecutions of boys under 17.

If you are aged 17 or over, you could be sent to prison for up to two years if you are convicted of unlawful sexual intercourse with an under-age girl. (The prison sentence could be longer if the girl was aged under 13). Provided you are under 24 and the girl was aged at least 13, you can defend yourself if you had reason to believe that the girl was actually 16 or over – provided, too, that you haven't been charged with this offence before.

If you and your girlfriend decide to live together, and she is under 16, you could be charged with taking an unmarried girl away from her parents. This can happen even if you don't have sex. If you are aged 17 or over, and are convicted of this offence, you could be sent to prison for up to two years. But prosecutions for this offence are hardly ever brought.

In theory, you could also be prosecuted if you take an unmarried girl *under the age of 18* away from her parents in order to have 'unlawful sexual intercourse' with her. 'Unlawful sexual intercourse' means sex outside marriage. (But don't worry: sex outside marriage itself is *not* a criminal offence). Your only defence is to show the court that you reasonably thought the girl was aged 18 or over. So, if your 17-year-old girl friend leaves home to live with you, you could be prosecuted, even though she is over the age of consent. Fortunately, prosecutions are almost never brought for this offence.

58

Boys under 16 can be ordered to a court to contribute towards a child's keep if they father a child.

Same-sex relationships

Homosexuality is sexual attraction to your own sex. About 10% of the population relate primarily to their own sex.

Many young people who will grow up to be lesbians or gay men experiment with members of the opposite sex when teenagers: just as many people have gay relationships when young and heterosexual relationships when adult.

Since the early 1970s there has been a gay liberation movement in which lesbians and gay men have come together to encourage gays to live their lives openly to help society accept homosexuality as a positive alternative and to campaign to combat discrimination.

In the last 15 years there has been a lot of change; there are now people in every walk of life (including MPs) who do not hide the fact they are gay, and many Trade Unions and some employers have anti-discrimination policies. However, gay people still don't get a fair deal from the law, for example the criminal law denies gay men equality with heterosexual men, and lesbian mothers are often denied custody of their children – regardless of how good they are as mothers and regardless of the wishes of the children.

Young gays sometimes get unfairly treated at school and it is possible for a young woman to be taken into care for being 'in moral danger' because of a lesbian relationship. If you are in the armed forces you can be punished for having a lesbian relationship. There is now an organization called the Lesbian and Gay Youth Movement (LGYM, London WC1N 3XX Tel. 01-317 9690) – so, if you're having a hard time, want to campaign or just want to meet other young gays you should contact them.

Girls and women in lesbian relationships

Lesbian relationships are not recognised in law and have never been illegal. There was an attempt to bring in a law in the 1920s but this was rejected. One MP said 'it would encourage ladies to do things which otherwise might never have entered thier minds.'

If you are both over 16, your relationship is lawful. The only way in which your relationship can infringe the law is if one partner is 16 or over and the other is not, in which case it would be technically possible to bring a prosecution for indecent assault or gross indecency. In practice these are seldom or never brought.

Boys and men in homosexual relationships

The law as far as gay men is concerned is very unfair. Although heterosexuals and lesbians can have sexual relationships quite legally from the age of 16, gay men cannot have relationships until they are 21 without breaking the law. Of course many people ignore this law and the vast majority of relationships never come to the notice of the police. However, it's sensible to know what's legal and what isn't. . . .

It is illegal for you to have a sexual relationship with another boy or man until you are *both* 21. Even then, homosexual behaviour is only legal when it is between only two individuals, when both of you are aged 21 or over and consent, and it takes place in private.

Any homosexual relationship which doesn't fit that definition can be punished by the law. Someone involved in a homosexual relationship could be charged with any of the following offences:

Buggery. This means anal intercourse, however slight. It is an offence to have anal intercourse unless you are both over 21 and it takes place in private and you are not in the armed forces. You can be charged with this if either or both of you are under 21, or if the act is not in private, or if one partner does not consent, or is 'severely subnormal'.

Gross indecency. This covers any homosexual act between males, other than buggery. It is most often used where the police say the act was not in private (e.g. in a public lavatory, even behind closed doors) or if one or both of you is aged under 21. It includes mutual masturbation, or one of you masturbating the other. In 1976, 14 boys aged under 17 were prosecuted for indecency.

Indecent assault. A man can be charged with indecent assualt if his partner is under 16 (a boy aged under 16 is assumed incapable of consent), or if his partner is aged 16 or over but did not consent. 'Indecent assault' can include a wide range of acts, from just touching to buggery. It is not an indecent assault to invite someone to touch you.

Importuning. If you repeatedly try to pick up another boy or man in a public place, or approach more than one other person, you can be charged with 'persistently importuning for an immoral purpose' – in other words, soliciting. In practice, the police usually only arrest people for this in places well-known for pick-ups.

When you can be charged with a homosexual offence

Whether or not you or your partner are prosecuted for homosexual behaviour depends on how old you each are, the circumstances in which the act took place, whether you both consented and so on.

If you are under 14, the law presumes that you are incapable of sexual intercourse. So you can't be prosecuted for buggery, though you can be prosecuted for *indecent assault* (if you are over 10).

If you are under 16, the law assumes that you are incapable of consenting to a homosexual relationship (just as it assumes that girls under 16 are incapable of consenting to a heterosexual relationship). Your partner, if he is older, could be prosecuted for indecently assaulting you or possibly for buggery, even if, in fact, you consented. If you touch or have sex with someone who is also under 16, or someone older who doesn't consent, then you could be prosecuted yourself for indecent assault.

If you are under 17, you could be taken into care on the grounds that you are in 'moral danger' because of your homosexual relationship. Or you could be placed under a supervision order, so that a social worker keeps an eye on you while you go on living at home. Obviously this won't happen if the local council's social workers don't find out about it, or don't think it is serious

60

enough to justify taking you into care. (See chapter 3 for more on care and supervision orders).

If you are aged 16 or over, both you and your partner can be prosecuted for gross indecency or buggery. (The Director of Public Prosecutions has to give his consent to a prosecution involving a homosexual man under 21. This does not often occur.)

Below we set out the *maximum* punishments which someone aged 17 or over could get for a homosexual offence if their case is heard in a Crown Court. The penalties in magistrates' courts are much less severe. The penalties for someone aged under 17 are set out on pages 98-103.

Gross indecency: two years' prison and/or a fine if you are both under 21; five years' prison and/or a fine if one of you is under 21 and the other 21 or over. The most common sentence is a fine.

Indecent assault: 10 years' imprisonment and/or a fine.

Importuning: two years' imprisonment and/or a fine.

Buggery: life imprisonment and/or a fine if your partner is under 16. If you are both aged between 16 and 21 and both consented, the maximum is two years' prison and/or a fine. If your partner was aged 16 or over but did not consent, the maximum is 10 years' prison and/or a fine. And a man aged 21 or over who commits buggery with a consenting man aged between 16 and 21 can get up to 5 years' prison and/or a fine.

If you are a young person whom the police suspect of having a relationship particularly with someone older, you can refuse to be medically examined or to answer police questions.

At the end of this chapter, on page 66, we list a number of organisations which give advice and support to homosexuals.

Contraception: girls and young women

The age of consent doesn't stop some girls and young women under 16 sleeping with their boyfriends. If you are thinking of sleeping with your boyfriend, it's a good idea to try and get advice on contraception.

If you are under 16 but at least 13 years old, you can get birth control advice and supplies from your doctor or local family planning clinic without your parents necessarily being asked for their permission or being told about it if the doctor feels that you fully understand the implications of what you are asking. Doctors and family planning clinics don't have to get this parental consent if they feel that your case is 'unusual' – which doesn't mean that your situation has to be particularly 'unusual', for example: it might simply mean that your parents won't or can't give adequate support and would only be angry or hurt if they knew you were getting help from someone else; or if it was a matter of incest (sexual intercourse with your father, brother, half-brother, uncle: see page 65) you would be unlikely to want your family to know that you were getting outside advice or treatment.

Your situation will be called 'unusual' if:
- you really don't want to tell your parent/s
- it's best for you to get advice and/or treatment although your parent/s don't know
- you understand the advice you're asking for

– you are likely to have sex without contraception
– you are likely to suffer physcially or mentally if you don't get any advice and/or treatment

This definition of 'unusual' was made up by the Law Lords in October 1985. Between December 1984 and October 1985, it was **Mrs Gillick** who had her way. She had complained that she, as a parent, should be asked *before* any advice or treatment was given, and the court of appeal agreed with her. This meant that, for ten months, not only did doctors and family planning clinics need parental consent to prescribe any form of contraception, but they also needed parental consent just to give advice. This resulted in many young women being prevented from seeking advice and treatment because they were afraid their parents would find out. During these ten months, only some 'emergency' cases should be dealt with without parental consent – for example, prescriptions for post-coital contraception (the 'morning-after pill'). Do you think parents should have had this control over their daughters' bodies?

Although Mrs Gillick has lost her case, the argument continues, and the Health Minister has reviewed DHSS guidelines (rules for doctors and family planning clinics to follow) which may result in a stricter definition of when advice and treatment can be given.

If you are aged 16 or over, it is completely up to you if you don't want to tell your parents that you are getting advice and/or treatment. There is no law that your parents should know. If you are under 16, it will be up to the doctor to decide whether you can consent to the treatment, and whether it is in your interest to prescribe contraceptives.

Contraceptives from a clinic or on prescription are free. Not all contraceptive measures have to be obtained by prescription. Sheaths for example can be bought without prescription.

The most common forms of contraception for women are the pill, the IUD (intra-uterine device or coil) and the cap. At the end of the book we suggest some organisations which can give you more information.

Contraception: boys

Most forms of contraception so far developed are for use by girls. The exception is the condom or sheath (Durex) which can be easily bought at most chemists and barbers and is not expensive. Don't take the risk of making your girlfriend pregnant: either make sure she is using contraception, or use it yourself. Men can be sterilised (the operation is called a vasectomy), but it is very unusual for this to be carried out on a boy or young man.

Pregnancy

If you think you're pregnant, find out quickly. If you decide you do not want to carry on with the pregnancy, you will need to arrange an abortion as soon as possible. If you do decide to keep the child, then the sooner you start planning the better.

If you are under 16, you may not want your parents to know you are pregnant. You can go to your family doctor for a pregnancy test but as with contraception s/he may have to tell your parents before giving you any advice or treatment. In practice it seems as though this rule is being broken by some doctors who will at least confirm whether or not you are pregnant without telling your parents. If you don't want to go to your family doctor, you should go to a local family planning clinic (see end of the book).

Many chemists advertise pregnancy testing kits which you can use at home. A positive result means you're pregnant. A negative result means you may be pregnant, and you should go to a doctor or clinic to check. These pregnancy testing kits are not 100% reliable and it is always better to have the test done by your doctor or family planning clinic.

If you are aged 16 or over, you should go to your doctor or family planning clinic to find out whether or not you are pregnant. They will treat your visit as confidential and cannot tell your parents without your permission.

Having a baby when you're under 18

Apart from the ordinary problems which may occur when you're pregnant, a number of particular difficulties can crop up if you are under 18.

If you're still at school, you may be reluctant to keep attending. You should ask the Local Education Authority if they will provide you with a home tutor during this time. If you're under 16, the LEA has to make arrangements for your education.

If you're not married, you have legal custody of your child. If you want advice you should consult the National Council for One Parent Families, (01-267 1361) or Rights of Women (01-251 6577).

You are entitled to a variety of benefits from the state – look at the section for women on pages 48 and 49.

Finally, if you're living at home and your parents are being difficult about you having a baby, you can contact your local social services department (look them up in the phone book or ask your CAB, advice centre). If your parents throw you out, you may be able to go into care with your baby with the local authority's help.

Abortion

If you are considering ending your pregnancy, you should try and talk it over with someone you know and trust, and discuss it with your own doctor or a counsellor at one of the pregnancy advisory services listed at the end of this book. Again as a result of the Gillick case (see page 62) if you are under 16 your doctor will not be able to help you get an abortion or even advise you about one without your parents being informed.

If you decide on an abortion, you should have it as soon as possible. The later an abortion, the less safe it is. Menstrual extraction (which is a method of gently sucking out the contents of the womb after your period is late or within a few days of sex) has now been declared legal as a form of abortion. It can be done even before you know you're pregnant, when the foetus, if there is one, is hardly developed at all.

An abortion needs the consent of two doctors. If your own doctor is unsympathetic, you should immediately contact one of the abortion advice agencies mentioned on page 66. About half of all abortions are done on the National Health, although married women are more likely than single women to get an NHS abortion. The rest of abortions are done privately, many of them through non profit-making charities. A private abortion in a non-profit-making clinic will cost about £80, although the price may be reduced if you can't afford it. If you are under 16, you need your parents' consent to an abortion. But the clinic must not check up on your age.

Living together

If you are aged under 18, you can live together as long as your parents or legal guardians don't object. If they do, they can stop you living together by having you made a ward of court (see page 13) or complaining to the police or the local council, which might end up with the girl being taken into care.

Once you reach the age of 18, you can live where you want to, and with the person or people you choose.

The legal and practical disadvantages and advantages of living together or getting married are set out in *Women's Rights: A Practical Guide* (see page 65 for booklist).

Marriage

If you marry when you are under 16, then the marriage will be void, in other words not recognised by law, unless you are married abroad in a country which has a lower age limit.

If you are 16 or 17 and want to marry, you need the written permission of your parents or legal guardian (or the local council if you are in care) if you are being married in a registry office. For a church wedding, you don't need their consent, but the banns have to be read for three consecutive Sundays without any objection. In Scotland you don't need any permission once you're 16.

If your parents or guardian refuse to consent to your marriage, you can apply to the local County Court for permission to marry. You should see a solicitor about this, or go to the clerk's office at the local court (look in the phone book) for information. If you try to get married without your parents' or guardians' consent, they could apply to have you made a ward of court, in which case you will need the permission of the court to marry. If you do manage to get married without their consent, then, provided you're aged over 16, the marriage will be legally valid.

Rape

A man or boy aged 14 or over, who has sex with a girl or woman who does not consent and the man knows that she didn't consent, or doesn't care whether she consents or not has committed rape.

If you submit to sexual intercourse because you have been threatened or given drink or drugs, then you have not legally given your consent, and the man can be found guilty of rape.

A boy under 14 cannot be prosecuted for rape, although he can be prosecuted for indecent assault. The maximum adult penalty for rape if life imprisonment. The sentences for boys under 17 are set out on pages 98-103.

The legal definition of rape only covers sexual intercourse (i.e. penetration of the penis into the vagina, however slight). Other forms of sexual assault are not, in law, rape: the man could be charged with indecent

64

assault (maximum adult penalty two years' imprisonment or five years if the girl is under 13) or with causing grievous bodily harm, or a similar offence.

Rape is particularly horrible and embarrassing for the victim. If you have been raped or sexually assaulted, whether recently or years ago, you can contact the Rape Crisis Centre on 01-837 1600 (24-hour phone) or 01-278 3956 (office hours) and they can provide free advice, help and support.

Incest

Incest means sexual intercourse, between close relatives for instance, father and brother (i.e. two people with the same mother but different fathers, or vice versa) is also incest. Sex between cousins is *not* incest. Homosexual incest does not exist in law. Although very few people are prosecuted for incest (mainly fathers accused of having sex with their daughters), it is rather more common than generally realised. Sexual acts which do not amount to sexual intercourse are not classified as incest but may still be against the law – see indecent assault (as above).

If your father or another relative is forcing sexual attentions on you, you don't have to put up with it. You can get in contact with New Grapevine (address and phone number is on page 66) and talk to them about it. They won't tell anyone (parents or police) about your situation unless you want them to.

Further information

Many books on sex are uninformative or written in a very patronising way. You may find these useful:

Make It Happy by Jane Coussins; a sensible book on sex education, written in ordinary language and full of practical help (Penguin, £2.95).

Our Bodies, Our Selves, edited by Angela Phillips and Jill Rakusen; a book on health and sexuality for women, originally published in the USA but revised for this country (Penguin, £7.95)

Women's Rights: A Practical Guide by Anna Coote and Tess Gill; full of facts and background information including a useful chapter on sex and the law (Penguin, £3.95)

Learning to Live with Sex good short pamphlet (Family Planning Assocation)

Homosexuality and the Law NCCL factsheet 15p plus s.a.e.

Maternity Rights at Work by Ruth Evans, Lyn Durward and Jean Coussins (NCCL, £1.50).

Pregnancy Month by Month and **New Born Baby** (Consumers' Association; £5.95 each).

The Law and Sexuality a guide for lesbians, gay men, transvestites and transsexuals. (Grass Roots Books, 1 Newton Street, Manchester 1, £1.00).

Helpful organisations

British Pregnancy Advisory Service, Guildhall Buildings, Navigation St, Birmingham 2 (021-643 1461) and 7 Belgrave Road, London SW1 (01-222 0985); run a number of advisory clinics and nursing homes.

Brook Advisory Centres, 233 Tottenham Court Road, London W1 (01-580 2991), specialises in helping younger girls and has centres in Coventry, Bristol, Birmingham, Cambridge, Liverpool and Edinburgh (addresses in local phone books). Completely confidential. You can phone, write or drop in.

Campaign for Homosexual Equality, 274 Upper Street, London N1 (01-359 3973), information about gay, transvestite and trans-sexual groups.

Family Planning Information Service, 27 Mortimer Street, London W1 (01-636 7866)

Family planning clinics, local clinics should be in the phone book under 'F'.

Friend, 274 Upper Street, London N1 (01-359 7371), information and support for homosexual and bisexual men and women. 7.30pm – 10pm every day

Gay Teenage Group, contact Gay Switchboard for local address.

Lesbian and Gay Switchboard, (01-837 7324); 24-hour telephone information service for gay people.

Lesbian Line, BM Box 1514, London WC1 (01-837 8602), telephone advice service. for lesbians.

National Council for One-Parent Families, 255 Kentish Town Road, London NW5 (01-267 1361)

New Grapevine, 416 St John Street, London, EC1 (01-278 9147)

Pregnancy Advisory Service, 11-13 Charlotte Street, London W1 (01-637 8962), another non-profit-making organisation which gives counselling and arranges abortions.

Release, 169 Commercial Street, London E1 6BW (01-837 5602); can give advice on legal problems, abortions etc.

7
ALCOHOL AND OTHER DRUGS

The word 'drugs' covers a wide range of substances. Some are legal, some are not. The most common everyday drugs are tannin, found in tea, and caffeine, found in coffee. Nicotine, in cigarettes, is highly addictive and dangerous, and alcohol can also be a killer, if taken in large enough quantities. The laws on drugs are inconsistent and confused.

Alcohol

It is often said that young people under 16 cannot drink alcohol legally. This isn't true. The law says that it is an offence to give alcohol to a child under five unless it is given by a doctor on health grounds. Between five and 16, you are allowed to drink alcohol provided that you do so on private premises.

It is against the law for anyone aged under 18 to buy alcohol from pubs, off-licences or shops. Both you and the person selling you the alcohol can be fined up to £200. It is also againt the law for anyone under 14 (apart from the landlord's own child) to go into a pub or licensed premises used for selling

The word 'drugs' covers a wide range of substances. Some are legal, some are not

and consuming alcohol. Once you reach 14, you can go into a pub but you can't buy or drink alcohol there. At 16, you are allowed to have beer, wine, cider or perry with a meal in a hotel or restaurant. At the age of 18, you are entitled to buy drinks in a pub and drink there.

Cigarettes

It is not illegal to smoke in private at any age. But it is an offence to sell tobacco, cigarettes or cigarette papers to someone aged under 16. You can also be taken to court if you are aged between ten and 16 and try to buy tobacco for your own use.

If you are under 16 and you are found smoking in a public place, a uniformed police officer or a park-keeper can seize all tobacco and cigarette papers (but not a pipe or tobacco pouch!)

Teachers may tell you that it is illegal to smoke before you are 16. It isn't – although the school rules may forbid it.

Illegal drugs

It is illegal to use, possess or supply certain claffified drugs. We give below the maximum *adult* penalty which applies for offences involving each class: see pages 98-103 for sentences which apply to young people.

Class A

These are the drugs considered to be most dangerous. An adult convicted of possessing any of them can be sent to prison for up to seven years. The police only have to prove that you were in possession of the drugs; it doesn't matter whether you had actually used them or intended to. The main Class A drugs are: heroin, cocaine, opium, LSD (acid) and injectable amphetamines.

Class B

These drugs aren't considered quite as dangerous as Class A but sentences are still high (five years' imprisonment and/or an unlimited fine is the maximum for an adult convicted of possession). The main Class B drugs are most amphetamines and amphetamine-related drugs, purple hearts, cannabis (both marijuana and hash), benzedrine and dexedrine.

Class C

This is the least serious group, although the maximum penalty which can be imposed on an adult for possessing a Class C drug is still two years and/or an unlimited fine. The main Class C drugs are Mandrax and similar stimulants.

The Advisory Council on the Misuse of Drugs Act has recommended that cannabis become a Class C drug, and Mandrax a Class B drug.

There are many other substances which people take in some way to try and get 'high'. These are things like glue, aerosols or even fire extinguishers, all of which can be inhaled. In general these are all highly dangerous substances and can cause very severe damage to your body, especially your liver. Some of the chemicals in these substances are also carcinogenic (i.e. they cause cancer).

Selling illegal drugs

The penalties for selling illegal drugs are much higher than for possessing them. An adult found guilty of selling Class A or B drugs can be sent to

68

prison for up to 14 years and also be heavily fined. Selling Class C drugs can get an adult up to five years in prison and/or a heavy fine.

Glues and Solvents

It is an offence for a shopkeeper to sell solvent-based products to anyone under 18 if they know, or have reasonable cause to believe, that the products are to be abused, and not used for their normal purpose. Therefore, if purchases are made regularly from the same shops, or quantities are purchased, the shopkeeper should refuse to sell them.

Other offences

It is an offence to grow or try to grow a cannabis plant. It is an offence to allow your home to be used for people to smoke cannabis or opium, prepare opium or produce or supply any other illegal drug. It is a very serious offence to try and import illegal drugs into this country. And, if you are going abroad, the penalties for possessing or supplying cannabis or other drugs can be far more severe than in this country and it is very difficult to get out of a foreign jail!

Police powers

The police can stop and search you in the street if they have 'reasonable grounds' to suspect you have an illegal drug. They can also stop and search your car. They are not meant to stop you just because you have long hair or dress differently or are black, but in practice they often do.

If the police have reason to believe you have committed an offence under the Misuse of Drugs Act, they can ask for your name and address. If you don't give it; and if they think you have given a false name and address; and if they think you will not turn up at court, then they can arrest you without a warrant.

Normally you will be released on bail by the police for up to three weeks while any drug they've found on you is analysed. You will have to report back to the police station on a specific date and, if the analysis is positive, you will be formally charged.

The police can also search your home to look for illegal drugs if they have a magistrate's court warrant.

Information and advice

Release, Institute for the Study of Drug Dependence, and *Standing Conference on Drug Abuse, see pages 110-115.*

National Campaign Against Solvent Abuse, Box S13, 245a Coldharbour Lane, London, SW9 8RR (01-733 7330)

If you do not live in London there may nevertheless be a drugs advisory service in your area. To get help locally ask your family doctor, talk to a teacher, social worker, probation officer or Citizens Advice Bureau. The Standing Conference on Drug Abuse, have a full list of local services throughout the country.

8
THE POLICE

You may come into contact with the police for all kinds of reasons. You may go to the police yourself if you've been attacked or robbed. You may ask them the way to somewhere. They may think you've committed a crime and want to question you about it. They may want you to be a witness in a case against someone else. Or the police may decide you are at risk – perhaps because you're not being looked after properly at home – and decide to take you into custody for your own protection.

Most of this chapter is about what happens if you are suspected of committing a criminal offence. On page 84 we suggest what your parents or friends can do to help if you're arrested. On page 86, we discuss what happens to the victims of crime, particularly people who have been sexually assaulted or raped. And on page 85 we mention points to watch for if you are being questioned as a witness.

According to the law, you can only be charged with a criminal offence if you knew that what you were doing was wrong when you did it. In England and Wales the law doesn't consider that children under the age of 10 have this sense of what is wrong. If you are below this age of 'criminal responsibility', you cannot be charged with a criminal offence, although you can be arrested and cautioned and you could be held under a 'place of safety' order if the police think you are beyond your parents' control or at risk of being injured; you could also be taken into care. (More on place of safety orders on page 38.) Anyone aged ten or over can be charged with a criminal offence, although it is rare for someone under 12 to be prosecuted. About two-thirds of 10 to 13-year-olds picked up by the police, and one-third of those aged 14 to 16 are cautioned instead of being prosecuted. More about cautions on page 84.

New rules and laws relating to police powers have just come into effect. Although these new rules are supposed to make the law simpler and easier to understand, many people feel that the police will have too much power, and ordinary people will have too little protection from them.

In the streets

If the police stop you it might be because they are looking for witnesses, young people who saw something – for example, if they are investigating a road accident near a school or even the murder of a child in the area. In this situation it is obviously a good idea to co-operate as much as possible.

It is often hard to tell why the police have stopped you and you might find that they start by questioning you as a witness to something and end up by suspecting you – sometimes of another completely separate thing.

If you think the police suspect you of doing something wrong, it is best to say as little as possible. Anything you say can be used in evidence in court – and it is very difficult to disprove their version of what you said. It is usually sensible to answer simple questions like 'What is your name and address?', 'Where are you going?' or 'Where have you been?' But if they go on questioning you, ask them what it is about and what they suspect you of. If they won't tell you or you're worried about what may happen, just say firmly that you don't want to answer any more questions. You don't have to answer any questions you don't want to, and if you do agree to answer questions, you can always insist on getting legal advice first from Legal Aid or a solicitor. To help stop young people from being taken advantage of, the Children's Legal Centre wants there to be a rule that your parent/s, guardian or another responsible adult (not a police officer!) should be informed if you voluntarily go to the police station to 'help police with their enquiries'. But even now you can ask for someone to be there if you want them.

However angry or upset you feel, it's always a good idea to behave politely to the police.

If you are stopped it is best to behave politely to the police.

Police powers to stop you

The police do not have any general right to stop you in the street. But they are entitled to stop you if you are under 17 and they believe you are being ill-treated or neglected, exposed to moral danger or beyond your parents' control. This would apply, for instance, if you are found sleeping rough, staying out late, going to 'unsuitable' places and so on. The police can take you to the police station and may refuse to let you go home if they think you are at risk. But they must tell your parents or guardians why they are keeping you.

With the Police Act, the police also have more special powers to stop and search than before – they can even set up road blocks to stop traffic. A police officer can stop and search you if s/he has *reasonable grounds for suspecting* that you have on you *or* in the vehicle:
– stolen goods (before the Act the police could only stop and search for stolen goods in Liverpool, London, Manchester, Newcastle and some other major towns, but now they can do this throughout the country)
– a prohibited article. This can mean anything the court considers in the circumstances to be an offensive weapon (for example, anything from a flick-knife to an everyday pen-knife, a bunch of keys, or even a comb). It can also mean anything you have in order to steal, burgle, or obtain property by deception (for example, a piece of wire or foreign coins which might be used to cheat vending machines or obtain money from phone boxes)
– illegal drugs
– protected birds' eggs
– items connected with terrorism (papers or articles which could suggest that you're involved)

What are reasonable grounds for suspecting you?

If the police want to stop and search you they must *already* know what they are looking for – they can't just search you because you *might* be carrying something you shouldn't. Also they must have a reason for suspecting you've got what they're looking for – this means more than just a hunch and is the same level of suspicion needed to arrest someone. They can't stop and search you to find out why they've stopped you! The new code of practice which tells the police how they should behave says that it is no reason to stop you just because you're young or black or 'dressed in a certain way' or you have a 'particular hairstyle'.

Before being searched

If the police officer is not in uniform s/he must show you his/her warrant card. Whether in uniform or not s/he must tell you:
– his/her name and which police station s/he comes from
– what s/he is looking for and why
– that you can get a copy of the written record of the search if you want.

If the police don't tell you anything, ask them what they are looking for and why. Try and make sure that anyone who is with you stays to watch you being searched. You may need them as witnesses.

If the police officer believes that you are unable to understand what is being said, s/he doesn't have to tell you what s/he is looking for and why. So, for example, a young Asian with a limited knowledge of English and who recently arrived in this country won't have the opportunity to assess whether the police officer has good reason for searching him because he won't even be told what's going on.

How the search should be carried out

A police officer should only search for what s/he already thinks you have on you – so, for example, if you were seen hiding a bunch of keys (!) in one of your pockets then the police officer can search that pocket but can't go on to search the rest of your clothes for anything else you might have. If you are being searched in public you only have to take off your coat or jacket or gloves – you can keep your hat on. You might be asked to go to a nearby van or police station so a fuller search can be carried out in private – this doesn't mean that you can't take witnesses with you. You can only be searched by a police officer of the same sex as you. The police officer can use reasonable force to search you if you refuse.

After the search

Once the search is over you can go free unless you are arrested. You can only be detained for as long as it takes to carry out the search.

After the search the officer must write out:
- what s/he was looking for
- what reasons s/he had for thinking you might have what s/he was looking for
- exactly when and where the search was made
- whether anything, and if so what, was found
- whether someone was injured or anything was damaged because of the search

You can get a copy of this report if you ask for it within a year. The police officer must tell you this.

At school

The police should *not* arrest you or come and question you at school. If this is essential, they should ask the head-teacher's permission and they should only interview you with the head-teacher or another adult present. If you are arrested or questioned at school unnecessarily, you should make a complaint (see page 85).

What you can be arrested for

The police can only arrest you if they have a 'power of arrest'. The police have this 'power of arrest' for breach of the peace. This can be used if the police think that what you are doing will lead to a public disturbance. The police also have a 'power to arrest' if they:-
- suspect an *arrestable offence* has been/is being/is about to be committed;
- have a *statutory power of arrest;*
- believe one of the *general arrest conditions* is satisfied;
- require the *fingerprints* of a convicted person.

What is an arrestable offence?

Arrestable offences include: any offence which may be punishable by at least 5 years' imprisonment, for example, criminal damage, theft, burglary, unlawful possession of drugs, rape, causing death by dangerous driving, most offences of violence, murder and treason; offences which carry a penalty of less than 5 years, such as indecent assault on a woman, taking and driving away a vehicle, going equipped for theft or burglary. You can also be arrested if you try to commit any of these offences or if you are involved in the planning or if you go along with someone who commits any of these offences. You cannot be arrested if you are under 10.

Statutory powers of arrest

Statutory powers of arrest exist for: Public Order Act offences, driving whilst unfit or disqualified, offences of trespass, illegal entry and other offences under the Immigration Act, and certain offences under the Prevention of Terrorism Act (temporary provisions).

General arrest conditions

The idea behind this is that the police should use summonses more. A summons is a piece of paper sent to where you are staying to tell you what you have to go to court for, which court you have to go to, and when you have to be there. If the police used summonses more they wouldn't have to arrest so many people unneccessarily.

However, the new Act doesn't describe the situations when summonses should be used – it only tells the police when summonses *shouldn't* be used. The result is that rather than cutting down on the use of arrest, the Act gives the police extra powers of arrest.

The general arrest conditions (reasons why you can be arrested rather than summonsed) don't relate to the seriousness of what you might have done but to your 'circumstances' at the time: where you are living, what you are likely to do.

1)   You don't have to tell the police where you are living or what your name is if you've been searched or if you are stopped and asked questions on the street. However, you might be getting yourself into trouble if you don't give them this information. For example, if the police think you've committed a small offence like dropping litter, illegal parking, or unauthorised collecting for charity and they want to prosecute you for this offence then they'll ask for a name and address where they can send the summons. If the police officer can't find out what your name is or thinks that the name given is false, or thinks that you won't stay at the address which you've given long enough for a summons to be served and there isn't an address where someone else (for example, a social worker) will accept a summons for you – if any of these apply then s/he can arrest you.

These conditions mean that young people who are homeless or living in temporary accommodation are more likely to be arrested than other people. Do you think that this type of arrest which makes young people more angry and frustrated is the only way of dealing with minor offences?

2)   You can be arrested for very small offences if the police officer thinks this is necessary: to protect a child or other vulnerable person; or to prevent

74

you from causing harm to yourself or others, damage to property, an offence against public decency, or an unlawful obstruction of the highway. The obstruction of the highway condition would allow the police to arrest you if, for example, you were on a demonstration or a picket handing out leaflets *and* refused to move on when asked to by the police. If two women had just parked their bikes on the pavement before going for a walk in the park, *and* the police officer who noticed this thought they were likely to kiss each other on their walk, then s/he could arrest them for illegal parking in order to prevent an offence against public decency.

Fingerprints

The police can arrest someone convicted of a 'recordable offence' (i.e. an offence which may be recorded in the national police records, which means most offences) in order to take their fingerprints. But only if all the following conditions are satisfied:
- the person was never kept in custody at a police station;
- fingerprints weren't taken at the time;
- within one month of the conviction s/he was asked by the police to go to a police station to be fingerprinted and after at least seven days s/he hasn't turned up.

Arrest with a warrant

In addition to the situations just listed, the police can also arrest people if they have a warrant for them. A warrant is a piece of paper granted by a magistrate, giving the police the power to arrest someone. If you are being arrested under a warrant you should check to see that you are the person named on the warrant. You should also check to see whether it says you should be released on bail. More about bail on page 83.

If you are arrested

If the police decide to arrest you they must tell you that you are under arrest and why you are being arrested even if this appears to be obvious. If they don't tell you, ask. They should caution you as soon as they arrest you, by telling you that you do not have to say anything unless you want to, but anything you do say may be taken down and used in evidence. Your right to silence applies even when the police don't seem to be asking you directly about the offence – for example, everything you say on the way to the police station will be noted down and can be used in court. The only exception is if you are arrested under the Prevention of Terrorism Act – you could then be prosecuted if you refuse to answer relevant questions.

Once you have been arrested the police can search you if they think you:
- are a danger to yourself or others
- have on you evidence relating to some offence
- have on you anything which could be used for an escape

This means you will probably be searched as a matter of course. As with stop and search in the street only your overcoat or jacket, and gloves can be taken off if the search takes place in public. If the police find anything which relates to these reasons for searching you they can take it.

The police can also search the place where the arrested person was at the time of, or just before, his/her arrest to look for evidence of the offence for which s/he was arrested. If the offence was 'arrestable' (see page 74) then the police can search any property which the arrested person lives in or controls in order to find evidence to do with that offence or another related offence.

At the police station

Your custody record

The details of what happens to you 'in custody' (while you are being held by the police) must be written down in the 'custody record'. There will be a 'custody officer' at the police station whose special job is to keep this record. S/he must not be involved in the investigation and has a duty to make sure you are treated properly according to the rules. When you arrive at the police station, the custody officer has to decide whether there is enough evidence to charge you straight away, and if there isn't whether you should be kept for questioning. If you are kept for questioning you'll probably have to turn out your pockets, since the custody officer has to make a record of everything you've got on you. S/he should tell you and make sure that your parent or guardian is told that you've been arrested and why and where you are being held. S/he should tell you and give you a written notice of your rights: to have someone else (as well as your parents) told of your arrest; to talk with a solicitor; to have a look at the rules which say how you should be treated. S/he has to write down every request you make to see a solicitor, and if you aren't allowed to see one, the reasons why not also have to be written down. Also if you ask the police to let someone else know of your arrest and the police don't allow this, the reasons why not have to be written down in the custody record. If your fingerprints are taken without your consent or if body samples are taken from you, the reasons why have to be noted in the custody record. You can get a copy of your custody record if you ask for it afterwards.

If you are searched

A written record of everything you have on you has to be made, so you might be searched when you arrive at the police station. This shouldn't mean a strip search unless the custody officer thinks this is absolutely necessary to remove something you wouldn't be allowed to keep, for example, evidence or a weapon. The reasons for a strip search have to be put on the custody record.

You can only be searched by someone of the same sex as you and no-one else other than a doctor should be present. The police can take anything they find, but they can't take your clothes or personal things unless: they can be used as evidence or to interfere with evidence; or if they could be used to hurt yourself or others or to damage property or for escape. The police must tell you why anything is taken. If you believe a search is simply to frighten or humiliate you then you can make a complaint later (see page 85).

In exceptional cases under the new rules a senior police officer will be able to authorise an even more intrusive search, including examination of the most private parts of your body. Such searches will only be allowed if there is real evidence to believe you have hidden drugs or a weapon which could not possibly be found any other way. A search for drugs can *only* be carried out by a doctor or a nurse at a hospital, surgery or other medical premises. The British Medical Association has indicated that doctors will not carry out such searches if the young person doesn't consent. But a search for a weapon can be carried out at a police station and, if there isn't a doctor or nurse available, it can be carried out by a police officer of the same sex.

Either a parent or a guardian or someone from your care authority or a social worker (who you may not know) or another responsible adult, who is the same sex as you, must be present during the search unless you do not want them to be, and they agree. The definition of 'responsible adult' here doesn't include police officers!

What support do you get in the police station?

If you are under 17, or you are (or police believe you are) mentally ill or mentally handicapped, the police must tell the adult who is responsible for looking after you (parent, guardian or local care authority) about your arrest as soon as possible. They should also ask this adult to come and see you.

At each police station you may be moved to, you also have the right to have someone else told of your arrest. However, if you've been arrested for a 'serious arrestable offence' (see page 82), the police may decide not to tell this other person for 36 hours if they think it would get in their way because it would:
- interfere with evidence, or,
- lead to harm to others, or,
- alert other people suspected of a serious arrestable offence, or,
- hinder the recovery of stolen property

If the police don't get in contact straight away with whoever it is you want told then they must tell you why and this reason has to go on the custody record.

The right to talk to and get advice from a solicitor whenever you want can also be delayed for 36 hours if the police think it would get in their way for the same reasons as above. You must be told why you aren't allowed to see a solicitor and this reason has to be noted. The police should tell you about these, your rights to support and advice, but they don't have to.

Questioning

It might be some time before you get any support at the police station – the adult responsible for you might not get there straight away and the police might delay getting you a solicitor or anyone else you might want to see. If you don't get to see anyone else (parent/guardian, friend, solicitor) for a while, this doesn't mean that they aren't trying to get support to you.

While you are waiting, the police may start questioning you or ask you to make a statement. You have a right to silence and don't have to answer any question or make a statement. Indeed if you have already asked for legal advice, the police shouldn't try and interview you at all until you've seen a solicitor unless you have agreed to this in writing or on tape, or unless the police think that if they waited to interview you then other people would be harmed or property would be damaged.

Even if you haven't asked for legal advice the police must not interview you or get you to sign a written statement unless an adult who is responsible for you is there. Once again the police don't have to wait if they think this would mean that other people would be harmed or property would be damaged.

Even if the police interview you in isolation because they think it would be dangerous to wait, or because they are breaking the rules, you still don't have to answer any of their questions. If they do get you to say things you don't mean, this can be used in evidence against you.

When the courts decides whether what you told the police can be used as evidence, they don't necessarily consider the situation you were in when you said what you did. It is less a matter of what you wanted to say, and more to do with how what you said fits into the rest of the evidence against you – whether 'reliable' or not. But what does reliable mean here?

Mohammed, who was 17, worked as a petrol pump attendant at a garage in West London. His employer accused him of taking money from the till and he was taken to the police station. After several hours' questioning, he confessed that he had stolen the money. But before the case came to court, his employer discovered that Mohammed was innocent: the money had been banked, and had never been stolen at all.

Colin Lattimore, who had mental disabilities, was arrested on suspicion of murder. He was 17 when this happened. He was questioned for nine hours in the police station, without his parents or anyone other than the police being present. He signed a confession statement admitting the murder. It was later proved that the murder took place at a time when Colin had an undisputed alibi: although he was innocent, he had been pressured into signing a false confession. He spent three years in prison before the truth was established.

Identification parades

You may be asked to take part in an identification parade if it is suspected that you are involved in some offence. You do not have to agree to this, but if you refuse the police may detain you and then have a confrontation with the witness. This means that they may just bring the witness into the room and ask him/her if you were the person involved. The witness may identify you mistakenly then because you have been arrested by the police and s/he may be tempted to think "there's no smoke without fire". Because of this it is often better to agree to a proper parade which is governed by various rules to protect you. Contact a solicitor if possible.

If you do agree to take part there must be an adult who is responsible for you present to make sure all the rules are followed. The other people in the parade must all be of roughly the same age and general description as you, including hair style and colour, clothing etc. You can choose where to stand in the line, and can change your place in the line in between witnesses. If you

have any complaint about the parade or think it is unfair in any way you should tell the officer who is in charge. S/he must make a note of this and, if you have been wrongly identified, this will help you in court.

Sometimes young people are asked to take part in identification parades where someone else is the suspect. Many people refuse to do this because of the inconvenience or a worry that they will be picked out and arrested themselves! However, by taking part in a parade you may be helping somebody to prove his/her innocence.

Sometimes the police hold confrontations instead of proper parades using as an excuse the fact that not enough people can be found to take part.

Your body. Fingerprints, photographs and body samples – how the police should behave

If you are between 10 and 14 it is up to your parents whether or not to let the police take your fingerprints or your photograph or body samples from you. If you are aged 14-17 then both you *and* your parent or guardian have to give consent. If you are 17 it is up to you alone. In each case the consent must be in writing.

Fingerprints

If you or your parents refuse to consent, your fingerprints may still be taken, using 'reasonable force' if necessary. This applies to anyone aged 10 or over. A senior police officer can only authorise this if you are suspected of an offence and your fingerprints may help you prove whether or not you committed this offence, or if you've already been charged with the offence, or told that you're going to be reported for it. You must be told the reason why you are going to have your fingerprints taken, and this reason must be written down in the custody record.

If your fingerprints are taken during the investigation of an offence, and you are not taken to court or cautioned about that offence, or if you are cleared of that offence in court, then your fingerprints must be destroyed. If you ask, you have a right to see them being destroyed.

If you have been convicted of certain offences, but did not have your fingerprints taken when you were arrested, you may have to go back to the police station and have them taken even after the court case is finished.

If you are being held under the Prevention of Terrorism Act (PTA) you have to give your fingerprints and let the police take your photo – and the police will probably keep these.

Apart from the PTA, photographs can only be taken without the appropriate consent (though force may *not* be used) where:
- the suspect is arrested at the same time as others and 'a photograph' is necessary to establish who was arrested, when and where;
- s/he is charged with or reported for a recordable offence and has not yet been released or brought before a court; or
- s/he is convicted of such an offence and his/her photograph is not already on record.

Body samples

The two types of body sample that can be taken from you are: 'intimate' body samples (samples taken from inside your body) which include blood, semen, urine, saliva, and genital or rectal swabs; and 'non-intimate' body samples, which include hair, nail scrapings, swabs from the surface of your body, footprints or body impressions.

Samples from inside your body can't be taken without the appropriate written consent (see above under fingerprints/photographs). Even then the police can't even get an 'intimate' sample unless a senior police officer has a proper reason for suspecting you of a serious offence (see page 82) and that the sample may prove whether or not you were involved. The reasons and what samples are taken must all be written down in the custody record. Samples other than urine and saliva can only be taken by a doctor, and all samples should only be taken when an adult responsible for you is there. If you are aged 13 or under and don't want to have them done even though your parent or guardian has given permission – then the doctor probably wouldn't try and take them since s/he could be prosecuted for indecent assault if s/he did so against your will.

'Non-intimate' samples can be taken without the appropriate consent by a police officer, but only if a senior officer authorises this for a proper reason, as above. The police must tell you beforehand what it is they think you've done which allows them to take these samples. This must all be written down in the custody record. Reasonable force may be used to get the samples, but an adult responsible for you should be there.

If nothing comes of the investigation of an offence, and body samples were taken, then they must be destroyed. If you ask, you have a right to see these samples being destroyed.

Being held without charge

The length of time that you are held by the police is measured from when you were arrested, or from when you first arrive at the police station, whichever comes first. If the custody officer decides there is enough evidence then you should be charged (see below page 82) straight away. If there isn't enough evidence the custody officer will decide whether to release you or keep you there without charge in order to get hold of or preserve evidence (prevent evidence they haven't got yet from being destroyed) or to obtain evidence from you by questioning. If the custody officer decides to hold you s/he must write down why and when this decision was made in the custody record. S/he must also tell you why you are being held.

In most cases (apart from serious arrestable offences, see below page 82) it is unlikely you'd be held for longer than 24 hours. Furthermore, after the first six hours and then every subsequent nine hours, a senior police officer should look at the reasons why you are being held and what has happened since you've been held in order to decide whether there is still a good reason for detaining you. At the end of 24 hours you have to be released or charged unless the police think you've committed a 'serious arrestable offence'.

What is a 'serious arrestable offence'?

The definition of 'serious arrestable offence' includes offences such as murder, manslaughter, firearm offences, rape and indecent assault which constitutes an act of gross indecency. It also includes any other offence which has already caused or is intended to or likely to cause: serious financial loss to anyone; substantial financial gain to anyone; serious injury to a person; the death of a person; serious interference with the investigation of offences or the legal system; serious harm to national security or public order.

If you are being held for longer than 24 hours

If you are suspected of a 'serious arrestable offence' you can be held for up to 36 hours before charge. Before a senior police officer gives permission for this, s/he must be satisfied that things are going as quickly as possible, and that it is necessary to detain you in order to get evidence. The senior police officer must write down why you are still being held and tell you the reasons. The name and rank of the senior police officer who makes this decision must also be written down in your custody record.

After 36 hours you can only be held if a Magistrates' Court decides there are proper reasons for still detaining you. A first magistrate's warrant can extend detention for up to 72 hours; if the police apply again, detention for up to 96 hours can be authorised. Each time your detention is looked at by the Magistrates' Court you have a right to legal representation; if necessary, the Magistrates' Court has to wait for you to get a solicitor before it can come to a decision.

How you should be treated

During your detention you should not normally be placed in a police cell if you are under 17 unless you are unruly or violent, and you must never be placed in a cell with an adult prisoner. You also have a right to be made reasonably comfortable and to be offered refreshments.

Being charged

Once there is enough evidence to charge you, the police cannot delay in doing so.

If you are under 17, the police will usually wait until your parents have arrived before charging you, even if your parents weren't allowed to be there while you were questioned. Being charged with an offence means that you will be tried in a court (see chaper 9 for more on the criminal courts).

When you are charged, the officer will caution you again. You will be asked if you want to say anything and again you don't have to. It is probably better to say nothing at this stage get legal advice first. After you have been charged, the police aren't allowed to question you any more about what you are meant to have done. But they will probably ask you about your background, school, exam results and so on, and note down details of your physical appearance.

After you've been charged

Once you've been charged with an offence the police *can't* question you any further about that offence, and must decide whether or not you should be allowed to go home on bail.

Bail means that you go free until the day set out for you to appear in court. As part of this bail the police may decide that your parent/s or guardian should put up a certain amount of money, which they would lose if you didn't appear at court on the right day.

You should only be refused bail if the custody officer:
- doesn't know your name and address or thinks you've given the wrong name and address
- thinks you might not turn up at court or might interfere with witnesses or obstruct police inquiries in some way
- thinks detention is necessary for your own protection or to protect someone else or their property from harm
- thinks it is in your interests to be detained, for example, you might be at risk if you go home.

If you are detained you must be transferred to the care of the local authority unless this is impractical or if you are a 15-16 year old young man *and* the police think you are 'unruly'. Local authorities must give you the advice and assistance necessary to someone in your situation.

After being charged, you must be brought before a court as soon as possible usually within 72 hours. If you haven't already been given bail, you, your lawyer or your parents can apply for bail at this first hearing, so that you don't have to go on staying in detention before your case is heard. See Chapter 9 for more on what happens at the court.

Making a note of what happened to you

If you have ever been in court, you may have noticed that police officers are allowed to refer to their note-books when they give evidence – provided they convince the magistrates that the notes were made at the time, or shortly after the incident.

You also have the right to use your notes to help you remember what happened when you were arrested and held by the police.

It can be months before your case is heard by the court and most people's memories fade quickly. So it is a great help if you are able to write down everything that happened – either in the police station if the police let you have paper and a pen, or as soon as possible after you are released.

If possible, try and write down what the police said and did; the name and number of the officer involved; what the police asked you and what you said (use the exact words as closely as you remember); what they took when they searched you or your home; what offence they said you were being charged with. Put the time and date at the bottom, and sign it.

Any notes you make at the time will be very useful for your lawyer. If you don't have a lawyer, you should take your notes along to the court with you, and ask the magistrates for permission to use them to refresh your memory of what happened.

Jumping bail

If you don't appear at court when you are meant to, then the juvenile court will probably issue a warrant for your arrest. It is an offence not to 'surrender to bail' (i.e. not to come to court after being released on bail).

Being cautioned by the police

If the police suspect you of committing a fairly trivial offence and you haven't been in serious trouble before, the police may refer you to the Juvenile Bureau. This is run by plain-clothes police.

Juvenile Bureaux differ from area to area, but basically they decide whether or not you are going to be prosecuted or just cautioned.

The officer at the Juvenile Bureau should:
– consider what the crime is that you are supposed to have committed,
– find out what your police record (if you have one) is like,
– visit your home to be able to take account of your home background,
– talk to your social worker, teachers, youth worker, probation officer, etc.

The whole process takes about four weeks. If there is very little evidence against you, the Bureau will probably decide that nothing should be done. If the reports they receive about you are bad, they will probably decide to prosecute. Otherwise, they will caution you. To caution you, the police must have as much evidence available as they would need for a prosecution.

Being cautioned means that you will have to admit committing the offence and you and your parents will have to go to the police station to listen to a stern telling-off from a senior police officer. Although a caution does not count as a conviction it *may* be mentioned in court if you appear there in future charged with another offence. For this reason, you should not agree to be cautioned if you are not guilty.

Helping someone who is being held by the police

If your child, or someone in your care, is being held by the police, you should be notified. (See page 76 for when an arrested person can have someone told of his/her arrest). If you haven't been told but think that someone you know is being detained, you should try to find out where they are by phoning round the local police stations (in the phone book under 'police').

If you are the parent of someone held by the police (or a social worker or teacher involved with the arrested person), you should go down to the police station and ask to be allowed in during police questioning. No-one under 17 should be questioned without a parent, guardian or another adult (who is *not* a police officer) of the same sex as the arrested person being present (the only exception to this is where delay may involve an immediate risk of harm to persons or serious loss of or damage to property.) If this is refused, you should make a formal complaint against the police.

You should also contact a solicitor or legal advice agency, or arrange for a lawyer to be present when the person who has been arrested is brought up in court. See page 90.

You may find that you get no help from the police you speak to, and that everyone denies having heard of the person you think has been arrested. Someone from an advice agency, or a solicitor, can help here and may get more co-operation from the police than you do.

Complaints against the police

You can make the complaint to the chief officer of police for the area. In London, S/he is called the Commissioner of Police; outside London, S/he is called the Chief Constable. S/he has to appoint an investigator (usually from an outside force or, in London, from a different division) to investigate your complaint. The chief police officer then decides whether or not to take disciplinary action against the police officer you complained about. In a criminal case, the investigator's report goes to the Director of Public Prosecutions who decides whether the police officer should be prosecuted.

There is also an independent *Police Complaints Authority,* which has to supervise the investigations of all complaints and occasionally intervenes in a serious case.

You should make your complaint in writing, directly to the chief officer. Keep a copy of the complaint, and ask for a copy of the statement you make to the investigating officer.

If the police are prosecuting you for a criminal offence, and you also want to make a complaint about the way they behaved, you should discuss this with your solicitor first. Your complaint is usually not investigated until after the case against you is heard.

You can get a leaflet about police complaints from the police station. NCCL also publish a fact sheet on police complaints (price 15p plus sae), as part of a series on people's rights and the police, *Know Your Rights* (price £1.50 plus 25p p+p) from NCCL, 21 Tabard Street, SE1 4LA.

If you are a witness to a crime

If, for instance, you see a car accident or if you are a witness to a robbery or attack, the police may want to question you to help them get evidence. They may simply take your name and address and contact you later. Or they may ask you to go to the police station immediately to give a statement. In order to do their job, the police need the co-operation of witnesses.

If you are under 17 and the police want to interview you as a witness, they should only do so if one of your parents or a teacher or your social worker or another adult of the same sex as you is present. You should tell them who you want to be present.

Witnesses have the same rights as people suspected of crimes. You don't have to answer questions or make a statement if you don't want to. Anything you do say can be used in evidence. What you say could be used to bring a prosecution against you, if it shows your involvement in any crime. Occasionally, witnesses are bullied by the police to say what the police want. Moussa, a 16-year-old boy, came to the NCCL after he had been kept in the police station for three days. He wasn't suspected of anything – but the police wanted him to make a statement about someone he knew who was suspected of murder. Eventually he gave the police the statement they wanted (although he says the statement was false), in order to get out of the police station. He claims the police said they would prosecute him for lying if he didn't tell them what they wanted to know.

If you think the police are beginning to suspect you, or if you think they're behaving unfairly, you should not say anything more to them until you have talked to a lawyer yourself.

Reporting a crime to the police

If you have been attacked or robbed, you will probably want to report it to the police. You should contact the local police station (in the phone book under 'police') as soon as possible.

The police will take details about you and about what happened. They will ask you for any information which might help identify the person who did the crime. Most people have very bad memories for people's faces and appearance, so it is important to tell the police only what you remember clearly and not to exaggerate.

If you have been raped, or sexually attacked or had a man expose himself to you, the police may be suspicious of your story. An article in the *Police Review* warned police officers that children and women complaining of sexual crimes might by lying in order to get someone into trouble or draw attention to themselves. But the police should be told of the attack, if possible immediately, at least in order to protect others. If you are the victim of a sex offence, you should only be questioned by a police officer who is the same sex as you. There is no legal obligation to report a crime, and many women and girls do not report rapes or attacks because they can't face being questioned or appearing in court.

The Rape Crisis Centre helps victims of sexual attacks. You can contact them on 01837 1600 (24 hour) or 01278 3956 (office hours) or write to PO Box 69, London WC1X 9NJ.

Victims of crime can apply for compensation to the Criminal Injuries Compensation Board, 10-12 Russell Square, London WC1 (01-636 2812).

9
THE JUVENILE COURT

The juvenile court deals with cases involving people under 17. This includes both criminal cases, where you are charged with an offence, and care hearings where the court has to decide whether or not the local council should take you into care. If you want to find you about care proceedings look at chapter 3. *This* chapter deals with criminal cases at the juvenile court.

Sometimes you can be tried in adult courts

The normal rule is that people under the age of 17 must be tried in the juvenile court. At the juvenile court, your case is heard by magistrates – there are usually three people, from the local community. There is no jury or judge at the juvenile court and you cannot choose to be tried by a jury.

But if you are charged with someone aged 17 and over, you may be sent either to the Magistrates' Court or to the Crown Court. If you've been sent to the Crown Court for trial, your case will be heard by a judge and jury. If your trial has already been heard at another court and you have simply been referred to the Crown Court for sentence, there will only be a judge there to decide the punishment.

You can be tried by an adult court if you are charged with a criminal offence together with an adult. Whether the case is heard at the adult Magistrates' Court or the Crown Court depends on how serious the offence is. If an adult is involved, there are certain offences (e.g. murder, rape, robbery) which can only be dealt with by the Crown Court.

Another difference between the two types of court is that you are more likely to be referred back to the juvenile court if you were initially sent to the adult Magistrates' Court rather than to the Crown Court. For instance, suppose you are sent to the Magistrates' Court for trial, perhaps you have been accused with an adult of stealing from a shop, and at court the adult pleads guilty and you plead not guilty – in this case you will be sent back to the juvenile court for trial. However, perhaps the offence is a 'serious' one, and you are being tried with an adult at the Crown Court – in this case, if the adult admits the offence and you plead not guilty, you *might* be sent back to the juvenile court for trial but not necessarily. As far as sentencing goes, if you are tried at the Magistrates' Court and are found guilty, you will still usually be sent back to the juvenile court for sentencing.

If a juvenile court is to be held in the same room as an adult court at least one hour must elapse between the two.

You can also be tried at an adult court (whether there's an adult involved or not) if you are charged with:
– murder, manslaughter, causing death by dangerous driving or any other offence involving killing someone. In this case, you must be tried at the Crown Court.
– a very serious offence, for which an adult could be sent to prison for 14 years or more.

Juvenile courts should only decide to send you to the Crown Court if they think that, if you are found guilty, you would need to be detained for a long time. It seems that some juvenile courts are more inclined to do this now than previously, especially where people are charged with robbery i.e. stealing with violence used. There have been some cases where young people charged with burglary have been referred to the Crown Court.

Going to court

There are three ways in which you may be brought before court:

summons – this is a written notice which tells you what offence(s) you are charged with and which gives the day and time that you have to be at court and the address of the court building. The summons may be posted to you or handed to you personally.

88

arrest – chaper 8 outlines the increased powers of the police to bring you before court by arresting you rather than by giving you a summons. After you've been held by the police you will usually be released on bail (allowed to go free) until the hearing of your case. The hearing date is shown on your copy of the bail paper and you will normally be given a charge sheet telling you what offences you have been charged with. For a 'serious' offence (see page 82 for what can be called 'serious'), the police might arrange for you to be kept in custody overnight and take you to the juvenile court the next day.

appearing as a witness or victim – this may be at a juvenile or adult court.

The hearing date

It is easy to forget dates. When you get the summons or bail paper, read what it says. It is best to put the paper in a safe place. Make a separate note of the date and time of the hearing and the address of the court and pin it up on the wall so it will not be forgotten.

If you don't turn up when you are supposed to, the case may be put off to another day, or a warrant will be issued for your arrest. You could also be committing the separate offence of 'failing to appear' for which you can be prosecuted whatever happens about the original charge.

If you can't make it to court, or aren't ready for your case

If you can't go to court – for instance, because you are ill – let the court and your solicitor know. If you haven't time to get a lawyer and prepare your case before the dates you've been given, write to the court asking them to change the date. If you don't hear from the court giving you a new date, you must still turn up on the date you've already got.

If you've been kept (locked up) in custody up until your appearance in court or if you simply haven't had the time to prepare for your case, you can on the day of the hearing ask for your case to be put off until a later date – this is called asking for an 'adjournment'. If your case hasn't been sorted out, you can go to the duty solicitor when you arrive at the court building. Duty solicitors are independent of the court and it is their job to give you advice and support and to represent you (stand up for you) in court if you want them to.

Getting help with your case

Always get a solicitor (lawyer) to speak for you in court. If you are going to plead 'not guilty' a solicitor can help you organise your case, so that your side of the story is put forward as clearly as possible in court. If you mean to plead guilty you should get a solicitor first, because the law is sometimes so technical you may be innocent without realising it, and with a solicitor you can find out if you have a (legal) defence to the case. If you do plead guilty, you need a solicitor to stand up for you in court and explain why you should be dealt with lightly – this explanation is called a 'speech in mitigation'.

If you are being held in custody (locked up) at a police station, it is important to get the outside support of a solicitor/lawyer as quickly as possible. What the police may have decided has happened and how they want things to turn out may not be the same as what you feel has happened – but without outside support it may be very difficult to resist their interpretations of events and to avoid being bullied into things against your wishes.

How to get a solicitor

If you have received a summons or are on bail, you'll need to find a solicitor for yourself. You may know one or have heard of one. Your parents or friends may suggest one. You can ask your nearest law centre or citizens' advice bureau (addresses in the phone book) to suggest one. You don't have to be shy about getting in touch with a solicitor. It is their job to take on cases and they will be paid by legal aid.

If you are locked up, you are allowed to make a phone call to your family or a friend. Ask them to get you a solicitor. If you are not allowed to make a phone call keep asking until you are. If you already have a solicitor, the police must contact them for you. If not, you can get the police to phone the local duty solicitor, who is available 24 hours a day to give you advice and support. Alternatively, you can choose a solicitor from a list of local solicitors which is available at the police station. If the police can't get in contact with the solicitor of your choice, they should try others until they get one for you.

Legal aid

Legal aid means that your lawyer's fees are paid by the state. If you get a summons by post, legal aid papers are sometimes sent too. If not, or if you are on bail, you should go straight to your solicitor or to the court office (there is usually a counter marked 'legal aid') and get legal aid papers from them. If either you or your parents have difficulty in understanding the forms, you can get your solicitor to help you fill them out. If you are under 16, the forms ask you how much money your parent/s or guardian have. If you are in care, your care authority isn't asked to give this financial information. Your parent/s or social worker should sign your legal aid form, but this is not absolutely necessary. If you are 16 or over, the forms ask you about how much income and savings you have, and it's up to you to sign them.

If you haven't got a solicitor by the time you appear in court

Some courts run a duty solicitor scheme. The duty solicitor will give you free legal advice and may speak for you in court. If you are at court and have not got a lawyer of your own, speak to the duty solicitor. There may be a sign in the court building telling you how to find the duty solicitor. Otherwise ask at the court office.

If you still haven't been able to get a solicitor by the time you get inside the courtroom, don't be afraid to ask the court to give you another future date when they can hear your case, so that you have time to find a solicitor – this is called asking the court to 'adjourn'. If the court thinks that you might get a custodial sentence (a sentence which involves being locked up) because it is a serious offence and you already have a police record, then the case will generally be put off for you to be advised and represented by a lawyer. However, if the case goes ahead without your asking for a solicitor then the court won't go back on its decision afterwards just because you weren't represented.

Bail

getting bail

If the court cannot hear your case on the day you appear, they can postpone ('adjourn' or 'remand') it to another day. If you admit the offence in court, or if you are found guilty, the case will usually be put off until a later date to allow the court to find out more about you. The magistrates will normally give you bail, which means you can go free until the date set for the next hearing. The court should only refuse you bail if it is satisfied that:
– you would not come back to court for your case,
– you would commit offences while on bail,
– you would interfere with witnesses or obstruct the course of justice,
– it is in your own interests to be kept in custody.
If you are waiting to be sentenced after your case has already been heard, you should be given bail unless the magistrates think it is necessary to place you in care for 2 or 3 weeks so that *full* reports can be made.

If the court gives you bail, they can also impose conditions – for instance, that you stay away from certain places or don't go out after a certain time of night. They can also ask for 'sureties', this means money which somebody you know, often your parent/s or guardian, promises to pay to the court if you don't turn up for your hearing, or if you break any of the bail conditions. £50 is the most that can be asked as a guarantee that you won't break the bail conditions. It is an offence not to turn up in court after being given bail, and the court can then issue a warrant for your arrest.

If conditions are imposed on your bail which you think are unfair, you can apply to a High Court judge to have them changed. You should talk with your solicitor for help with this.

If bail is refused

If the court refuses to grant you bail, they must remand you into the care of the local authority until your case comes to court again. You will then probably be sent to a community home. However, if the court defines you as 'unruly', you won't get bail. They might define you as unruly if:
– in the past you kept running away from a community home or you upset the running of a community home, or
– you've been charged with an offence of violence and have in the past been found guilty of an offence of violence, or
– you've been charged with an offence for which an adult could be sent to prison for more than 14 years, for example, robbery, rape, or murder.
Before making out an 'unruliness certificate', the court has to find out what the local council says. If the local council reports back that there is no suitable community home for you, then the court will probably send you to the nearest remand centre. If it is the first time that a case of yours has been

remanded *and* the court is satisfied that there hasn't been enough time for the local council to prepare a report, then the court can do without it.

If the court makes out an 'unruliness certificate' and has been told there is a remand centre available, then it can send you to the centre for up to 28 days. Remand centres are run by the Home Office, who run the prisons, so if no remand centre place is available to fulfil the function of control, you could be sent to prison.

If you are remanded in care or certified as 'unruly' and you think the decision is unfair, you can apply to a High Court or Crown Court judge for bail. You should talk with your solicitor for help with this.

Preparing your case

You can help your lawyer by telling him or her as clearly as possible your side of the story. You and the witnesses should talk to your lawyer as soon as possible while the details of what happened are still fresh in your mind. It might help your memory if once you get home you write down a note of what happened at the time of the alleged offence and afterwards while you were at the police station. It is important for your side of what happened to be heard in court, whether you plead 'guilty' or 'not guilty', because the police often have a completely different version of the events.

There are two types of information which your lawyer will bring up in court: information about precisely what happened at the time of the alleged offence which you and/or witnesses have provided; and information about your state of mind at the time of the alleged offence, about what you are like generally which can be provided by reports written about you, what people you know say about you in court, and how you come across when you're in court. If you plead 'not guilty' your solicitor will emphasise the details of what happened; and if you plead 'guilty' your solicitor will emphasise what sort of person you are.

Information about your state of mind at the time of the alleged offence can be useful to your solicitor whichever way you plead:- if you plead 'not guilty', what you meant or didn't mean to do at the time of the alleged offence may be crucial to your defence; 'intentions' can play a big part in legal definitions; and if you plead guilty, your solicitor may want to show that you weren't your usual self at the time of the offence.

Pleading 'not guilty'

Your solicitor will ask the police what evidence they have against you, and whether they will give you copies of their own witness statements. In more serious cases (including theft, serious criminal damage or assault, burglary etc.) the prosecution have to give you this information if you ask for it. The court will normally ask you if you have been told about this right. If you have not been told, or have asked for but not been given the information, the case will be adjourned because you are not properly prepared. However, you must ask for the information before pleading 'not guilty' in court. If you do not do so then, you may not receive the information later.

Although your own lawyer will prepare the case and interview your witnesses, it helps a lot if you put your witnesses in touch with him/her, and also make sure that your witnesses come to court when needed.

92

Pleading 'guilty'

If you plead guilty, the emphasis will be on why you shouldn't be dealt with too harshly. Preparation for this 'mitigation' would involve highlighting evidence of what your state of mind was at the time of the alleged offence, evidence of your character which is provided by what other people say about you. From this evidence your solicitor may be able to show that you acted 'out of character' when the offence was committed, for example, perhaps you were very upset about something at the time.

It is up to you and your solicitor what evidence will be presented in court to show what you are like. The evidence can be oral (people coming to speak up for you in court) or written (reports, references, or letters for the court). This character evidence can be provided by school reports if you are still at school. If you have a probation officer or social worker, and have told them about the case, they will either come with you to court or send a written report. If you are working and think your employers would support you, you can get a reference from them. You can also get any responsible people from your community who know you well to come and stand up for you in court, or if they can't come they can always write you a letter to be given to the court.

If compensation or a fine may have to be paid, the court will be impressed if you have saved some money and brought it along with you to show your willingness to make up for your offence.

How you come across in court

The sort of things that impress courts are:
- trying to be neat and tidy in your dress and appearance
- standing up straight and looking towards the magistrates
- not putting your hands in your pockets, it's best to keep them by your side
- not eating or chewing gum in court
- when you are speaking to the magistrates address them as 'sir' or 'madam'
- magistrates sometimes ask: 'Why did you do it?' Think about this and have an answer ready in case you are asked.

Getting to court

Try to get to court half an hour or so before the time given in the summons or bail paper. When you arrive tell an official you are there: if there is a window marked 'enquiries' or 'legal aid' give your name to them; sometimes an usher or court officer ticks off the names of people as they arrive. If you do not have a lawyer you should fill in the legal aid forms and see the duty solicitor as soon as you get to court.

If you are under 17 at least one of your parents or a guardian is supposed to come to court with you. If no-one comes along, the case may be put off until another day.

Calling of your case

The court officer has the court list for the day – they call out the cases as they come up. There may be a wait before your case is called – you could bring a friend to talk to or something to read. When your case is called, the court officer will show you and your parent/s or guardian into the court.

93

What's it like inside the courtroom?

Juvenile courts are meant to be informal, but some are more informal than others. Some are held in vast Victorian buildings, others in much smaller, modern buildings with fitted carpets and ordinary chairs. Sometimes juvenile courts are in the same building as the adult Magistrates' Court. But the law says that if a juvenile court is to be held in a room which is also used as a court where adults are tried, then there must be at least one hour's gap between the two sorts of cases.

Magistrates (sometimes called justices or 'the bench')

There are usually three magistrates. Most magistrates are people from the local community and are not paid for their work as magistrates. However, one of the magistrates at busier courts may be a paid one with legal training, called a 'stipendiary'. Stipendiaries can even hear cases on their own. The magistrates usually sit behind a large desk at one end of the courtroom, and one of them (usually the one in the middle) will do the talking for all of them. The magistrate's job is to make sure you understand what it is you are being charged with, and to decide whether you have committed the offence and, if you have, how you should be dealt with.

Justices' clerk

The clerk sits in front of the magistrates. It is the clerk who reads out the charge (the offence you are said to have committed) and asks you whether you admit or deny the charges. Justices' clerks are trained lawyers. They advise the magistrates on the law and are responsible for the day-to-day running of the court. But they have no say as to whether you are guilty or how you should be dealt with.

Lawyers

Your lawyers and the lawyers for the prosecution will usually sit to one side of the court. Often the police don't have a lawyer and their case is presented to the court by the officer who prosecuted you, or a court inspector.

Probation officers, children's officers and social workers

There is likely to be one of these people in court when your case is heard. They usually sit at the back, or on the other side of the court from the lawyers. If you admit the charge or the magistrates find the case proved, they may be asked to write a report for the court about you.

Press reporters

The public are not allowed to attend the juvenile court, but press reporters are allowed. Anyone else wanting to attend has to get special permission. This is different from the Magistrates' Court where anyone can attend.

Press reporters aren't allowed to print your name or address or the name of your school, or a photo or anything else which would tell people who you are. If you are under 17, this applies if you are a witness or victim in a case, as well as if you are actually being charged with an offence. Occasionally, however, the magistrates allow your name to be published – for instance, if you are a witness but there are rumours going round that you are the person charged with a crime.

Ushers or court officers
These people make sure the courts run as smoothly as possible: noting who is at court, calling the cases, and showing you into the courtroom. They often stand by the door at the back of the court.

Asking questions
The magistrates are supposed to help you understand what's going on. But if you don't understand, don't be afraid to ask. If you have difficulty speaking or understanding English, ask for an interpreter.

Understanding the charge
When you first go into court the clerk will read out the offence with which you are charged. You will then be asked whether you admit or deny it. Your solicitor should already have explained exactly what is meant by the particular charge. If they haven't, or you haven't had a chance to talk about it with them, it is worth checking what exactly is meant by the name of the offence you've been charged with. For example, part of the meaning of the charge 'theft' is that you *deliberately* stole something – so, if what happened was that you walked out of a shop without paying because you forgot to pay then you didn't *steal* anything. The magistrates have a duty to make the meaning of the charge clear to you. If, once you've heard what the charge means, you change your mind about how your case should be presented, you can ask for time to talk with your lawyer. Your case will then be postponed, probably to another day, to give you this time.

Admitting or denying the charge
Once the charge has been read out and you understand what it is you're being charged with, you can then do one of three things:

1.   You can ask for a postponement to give you time to talk to a solicitor about your case. If you are unsure what to do or if you have not spoken to a solicitor, it is best to ask for a postponement.

2.   You can deny the offence. The case will then most likely be put off until a later date when witnesses can be called by the prosecution to try to prove that you committed the offence. You will be able to call witnesses in your defence.

3.   You can admit the offence. You should not do this unless you have first discussed it with a lawyer or a duty solicitor. If you admit the charge you may be dealt with there and then. But usually the case will be put off until a later date to allow the court to find out more about you.

Defending a case
If you didn't do what you are accused of, or if your lawyer tells you that you may have a legal defence, you should deny the charge – clearly saying 'not guilty' or 'I didn't do it'. On the day of the hearing, the prosecution (usually the police) may bring any witnesses to court. The police officer or a solicitor employed by the police might start by explaining briefly what they think you did – this explanation is called 'speech'. They may go on to call a witness to tell the court what they saw or what they heard you say. A police officer may

give evidence of any verbal or written statement they say you have made. After a witness has finished answering police questions, your lawyer can ask questions. This is called cross-examination. You or your parents can ask questions instead. But you or your parent/s can get your lawyer to ask the questions you want asked, by telling him/her straight away if you disagree with any of the evidence brought against you. The magistrates may also ask questions.

When the police have called all their witnesses, you can put your case. Your lawyer may start by explaining to the court why you deny the charge. You or your parents could make this 'speech' instead if you prefer this. The way to put your side of the story is to give evidence – go into the witness box and answer your lawyer's questions. When answering, take your time and think about the question, and look towards the magistrates when giving your answer. The clerk or magistrates might also ask you questions to clear up things they don't quite understand. After you have given your evidence you can be questioned by the prosecution. If you do not understand the question, say so. Think before answering and keep your answers short. After you have been questioned, your own lawyer has a chance to ask you more questions to clear up any points.

You can call any other people who can confirm your story as witnesses: perhaps someone who was with you while you were dealing with the police, or perhaps someone who was with you at the time the offence was committed and who can confirm that you were somewhere else with them at the time (this is called an 'alibi').

You could also bring someone along to court to speak about your good character – a responsible person in your community who knows you. The prosecution can of course question you or anyone who stands up for you in court – so check with your lawyer first about who should stand up for you in court. For example, if you call a character witness, this may allow the prosecution to raise questions about your character.

If your lawyer didn't stand up and explain why you deny the offence before your evidence was presented and your witnesses were called, they can make this 'speech' afterwards. Perhaps they will summarise the evidence as part of this 'speech'. Very occasionally the magistrates will let you and the police make final as well as opening speeches.

Promising to tell the truth

Everyone who gives evidence has to promise the court that they will tell the truth. You will be asked to swear on the Bible to tell the truth, but you can instead ask to swear on the book of your own religion (perhaps the Koran or Bhagavita), or you can simply promise to tell the truth ('affirm') if you don't believe in swearing on a religious book. If the magistrates think you are too young to understand why swearing an oath should make you tell the truth, they may allow you to give evidence anyway, provided they think you understand that you have to tell the truth.

The decision

When the evidence from both sides has been heard the magistrates will probably leave the courtroom to discuss the evidence and come to a decision. When they come back into the courtroom you should stand up and remain standing while they give their decision.

They may say that they find the charge proved (find you guilty) or that they find the charge not proved (find you not guilty). If you are found not guilty on all charges ('acquitted') you are free to leave the court. If you are found guilty the prosecution will then tell the magistrates about your background, including whether you have had any previous convictions or formal cautions (see page 84). Cautions will usually be read out by a police officer. If you disagree with anything they read out you should tell your lawyer straight away. At that stage the magistrates will often ask for reports on you. The court can place a young person in care for two or three weeks so that full reports can be made. If the court decide to do this (see Bail, page 91) and you think the decision is unfair, you can talk with your solicitor about whether or not to apply to a High Court or Crown Court judge for bail.

Reports

These are usually prepared by a probation officer or social worker and will give information about your home and family background and your behaviour and progress at school. There may be a separate report from your school and sometimes a medical report. When talking to the probation officer and social worker remember that anything you tell them may be written down in the report. Don't forget to mention all the good things about yourself. If you know someone who will speak well of you ask for that person to be contacted.

Arguing for a lighter sentence

The argument for a lighter sentence is often called a 'plea in mitigation'. The kind of sentence you receive should depend on the information presented to the magistrates about you and your situation. You can work with your lawyer in order to get across what you perceive your situation to be.

When you come before the court for sentence you should ask your lawyer to let you see any reports that have been written about you and you should read these carefully and tell your lawyer anything that is wrong or that you feel is unfair. In some courts the reports may not be given to you but may be read out in court. The magistrates don't have to read out all of the reports, but if they don't, you can still insist on being read the relevant parts of the reports – the parts which would influence their decision. If you feel any part of a report is wrong or unfair, speak to your lawyer about it. Before the court sentences you, your lawyer has a chance to speak for you and to put to the magistrates any reasons why you should be given a light sentence – perhaps highlighting the relevant parts of the reports. If there are things in your favour or any special circumstances such as family problems which have been left out of the reports, ask your lawyer to tell the court.

Appeals

If you are unhappy about the result of your case you should discuss an appeal with your lawyer straight away. The appeal papers have to be filed in court within 21 days of your conviction or sentence in the juvenile court.

If you and your lawyer think you have been wrongly convicted (i.e. you shouldn't have been found guilty) then you can appeal to the Crown Court. If, as a result of the original conviction, you were given a 'custodial' sentence (i.e. a sentence which involves you being locked up) you may also want to apply either to the juvenile court or to the Crown Court for bail – so that you can be set free at least until your appeal is heard.

If you want to appeal against the kind of sentence you received then you can also appeal to the Crown Court. Once you've put in your appeal, usually nothing will be done about enforcing the sentence given by the juvenile court until the appeal is heard. The exception to this is, once again, if you have been given a sentence which involves you being locked up – in this situation you may want to apply for bail to be released until the appeal.

Sentences

There are many different sentences which a court can decide on for people under 17. They are briefly set out below:

1. Absolute discharge

This means that you are technically found guilty – but you don't have to pay a fine or serve a custodial sentence or anything else. It usually means that the magistrates think that the police should not have prosecuted you or that it would be unfair to punish you.

2. Conditional discharge

This is also a conviction without a punishment. But it can be held over you for up to three years. If you are convicted of another offence in that time, you can be given a punishment for the first offence as well as for the new one.

3. Fine

You can be ordered to pay a fine. The maximum amount of fine for any particular offence is fixed by law. The magistrates have to take into account how much money you have in deciding what sum to fine you. If you're between 10 and 13 years old you can't be fined more than £100. If you're between 14 and 16 the maximum fine is £400. Your parents are made responsible for the paying of the fine – so, if you can't pay it they'll have to. If neither you nor your parents can afford it at once, you can apply to pay in instalments.

4. Compensation Order

The magistrates can order you to pay up to £1,000 in compensation for each offence to the victim of the crime. The maximum compensation that can be ordered, if more than one offence has been committed, is £2,000. For instance, if you are convicted of burglary you could be ordered to pay the cost of replacing the window you broke in order to get in, as well as the cost of the goods you stole if these have not been returned.

A compensation order may be the only punishment you get, or it may be in addition to, say, a supervision order or one of the other sentences mentioned in this list. The court must make your parents liable to pay the compensation order.

5. Being disqualified from driving

The juvenile court can disqualify you from driving or holding a driving licence – even if you are too young to have a licence anyway. You will almost always be disqualified, in addition to any other sentence you may get, if you are convicted of taking and driving away another person's car ('TDA'). For other offences relating to motor vehicles, you will receive penalty points which will be endorsed on your licence. Even if you do not have a licence yet, the penalty points will be noted on any licence you apply for in the future.

6. Attendance Centre Orders

These are meant to provide a 'short, sharp punishment' for young male offenders. You can be ordered to an attendance centre if:
- you have broken a probation or supervision order, or if you have been found guilty of an offence for which an adult could be sent to prison (this includes most offences involving theft or violence); *and*
- you have not been sentenced previously to borstal training or any other form of custodial sentence (see points 9 and 10 below); *and*
- there is an attendance centre near enough for you to get to.

The magistrates will order you to go to the attendance centre for a set number of times. The total is usually 12 hours but can be less if you are under 14, or up to 24 hours if the court thinks that 12 isn't enough.

The magistrates may tell you which dates you have to go to the attendance centre. The sessions are usually held on Saturday afternoons and you will normally have to do physical training there.

If you don't turn up at the attendance centre, or you break its rules, you can be brought back to the court, which can send you to a detention centre or impose any of the other sentences mentioned in this list.

7. Supervision Order

This means that a social worker will supervise you for up to three years. S/he is meant to be able to advise and help you by keeping in regular touch with you. You are meant to co-operate with the social worker and see him/her regularly.

The supervision order may require you to obey certain particular directions specified by the court or given to you by the supervising officer. There may be a direction that you live in a particular place (usually your home) or take part in specified activities (for example, an Intermediate Treatment scheme) or attend particular appointments (e.g. for medical examination or psychiatric treatment). Such directions are limited to a maximum of 90 days during the period of the order. In addition, the court may impose a condition that you do *not* take part in a named activity (e.g. attending professional football matches) for a maximum of 90 days during the period, or a night restriction order (for a maximum period of 30 days during the first 3 months of the order.) A night restriction order is an instruction to remain in a certain place (usually at home) for specified periods between 6pm and 6am. These last two conditions can only be imposed in suitable circumstances and with your consent (if over 14) or that of your parents (if 14 or under).

If you fail to comply with any condition in the order you may be fined up to £100 or sentenced to Attendance Centre, although the supervision order will normally continue to be in force. If you don't co-operate with the supervision order the local authority may take you back to court to have the order replaced with a care order in certain circumstances. If you are over 18, and fail to co-operate, the supervision order may be revoked and you may be given an alternative sentence which could include a prison sentence of up to 6 months or a fine of up to £2,000. A supervision order made in care proceedings will end when you are 18 years old. In any other case it will last for a maximum of 3 years.

You can apply to have the supervision order ended. You might find it helpful to get advice from a solicitor about this. Your supervising officer will probably assist you in getting the supervision order cancelled if you are getting on well.

8. Binding over

Very occasionally, the magistrates may decide to bind either you or your parents/guardians over. This means that your parents/guardians, if they consent, have to pledge a sum of money up to £500 as a promise that they will take proper care of you and control you properly. They don't have to produce the money, but have to show they have enough to pay. If they don't manage to do this and for instance you are later found guilty of another offence, they have to give the money to the court. This must not last for more than three years, or until you are 18. If the court thinks the offence is a serious one, then you yourself can be bound over for up to a year to keep the peace and be of good behaviour. This means that you sign the bond – the maximum you can be asked to pledge is £50.

9. Care order

A care order means that the local council takes over the rights and duties of your parents, and can insist on your living in a community home. A care order normally lasts until you are 18. But if you are aged 16 or 17 when it is made, it lasts until you are 19.

A care order can be made if you are found guilty of an offence for which an adult could be imprisoned (e.g. most offences involving theft and violence or taking and driving away a vehicle).

Where a care order is made because you have committed an offence, the local authority's power to let you live with your parents or anybody else can be made subject to the control of the court. The court can only make such an order if it feels that the seriousness of the offence you committed justifies it and there is no other suitable way of dealing with you. It can only make such an order if you are legally represented or have failed or refused to apply for legal aid to get a solicitor. The order can only last for up to 6 months, except that if you commit another offence during that time the court can make another order. See chapter 3 for detailed information on care.

10. Detention Centre

If you are aged between 14 and 20, and you are found guilty of an offence for which an adult could be imprisoned, you can be sent to a detention centre. This applies to boys only – there are no detention centres for girls.

The normal length of time spent at a detention centre is 3 months, although the shortest is 21 days and the longest 4 months. You are entitled to remission of up to a third of your sentence for good behaviour during your detention.

Detention centres are meant to provide a 'short, sharp shock' in order to put you off a life of crime before you have acquired a serious criminal record. They are run on strict lines with an emphasis on hard physical activity. Because they are not suitable for someone who is physically or mentally unfit, the court has to get a medical report on you first. Recently the government has 'toughened up' detention centres to make life in them even harder.

When you leave detention centre, you will be supervised by a probation officer or social worker for up to 12 months.

Detention centres emphasise hard physical activity rather than education.

11. Youth Custody

If you are over 15 and under 21 and convicted of an offence for which an adult (defined as someone of 17 and over) can be sent to prison, you can be sentenced to youth custody for between 4 and 6 months for one offence or a total of up to 12 months for two or more offences dealt with in the Magistrates' Court. A Crown Court judge can send you to a youth custody centre for up to 3 years for serious offences, and if the Magistrates' Court thinks that its power and punishment are insufficient, it may send you to the Crown Court for sentence. Until the Crown Court hears your case, you can be sent to a remand centre or prison, or released on bail (see page 91).

At the Crown Court, you or your lawyer can make a 'speech' to the court explaining the circumstances of the offence and perhaps urging them to consider an alternative to youth custody. Before either the Magistrates' Court or the Crown Court sentences you to detention centre or youth custody, it must come to the conclusion that no other disposal of your case is appropriate, either because of the seriousness of the charge or because you are unable or unwilling to respond to non-custodial penalties. Normally social enquiry reports must be obtained before coming to such a conclusion, and you will be allowed legal representation.

12. Deferred sentence

The court can put off (i.e. defer) passing sentence on you, to see how you behave for the next few months. Sentence can only be deferred for a maximum of six months, and you have to agree. If you keep out of trouble in that time, the court will take this into account when you come back to be sentenced: but equally, if you commit other offences, they may give a more severe punishment for the original offence. If you stay out of trouble during the period of deferment, and comply with any conditions (for example, to attend school regularly) imposed by the court, then a custodial sentence should not be imposed when you return to court.

13. Hospital or guardianship order

If a young person under the age of 17 is convicted of an offence for which an adult could be imprisoned, and two doctors certify that s/he is suffering from mental illness, psychopathic disorder, subnormality or severe subnormality, the court may order him or her to be detained in a mental hospital. Alternatively, the court may order the local authority to become the person's guardian. If the magistrates think that there should be restrictions on the person's release from hospital, they have to refer the case to the Crown Court which can make a hospital order saying that s/he can only be released with the Home Secretary's consent.

14. Detention subject to the directions of the Home Secretary

If you are convicted by the Crown Court of a very serious offence, for which an adult could be sent to prison for 14 years or more – for instance, murder, rape, robbery or burglary – then the court can order that you be detained 'subject to the direction of the Secretary of State'. This means that you are detained on whatever conditions s/he decides. At first, this will probably be

102

in a youth custody centre or detention centre, community home or a youth treatment unit designed to deal with very disturbed children. But after you become an adult, you will probably be transferred to prison.

Legal costs

If you are found guilty, the magistrates may order you or your parents to pay part of the costs of the police in bringing the prosecution.

10
COMING OF AGE

We set out here a summary of your rights year by year. We've put in as much as possible, but we can't cover everything! More information on most of the points mentioned is given in other chapters.
You. . .

can have an account in your name with a bank or building society, or have Premium Bonds in your name;
can have a passport of your own, provided one of your parents or guardian signs the application form;
can inherit goods or money.

must go to school or other full-time education;
can drink alcohol legally;
see a U or PG category film (7 years old in London) but the cinema manager has discretion over admitting you.

can draw money from your Post Office or TSB savings account;

can be convicted of a criminal offence (but until you are 14, the prosecution has to prove you know the difference between right and wrong).

can buy a pet without a parent being present.

can get a part-time job so long as it is a 'light' one for not more than two hours per day or one on Sundays.

can:
be held fully responsible for a crime; be sent to a detention centre, if convicted of a crime (boys);
own an air rifle and, under certain conditions, a shot-gun;
go into a pub, but not drink or buy alcohol there (you can buy soft drinks);
play dominoes or cribbage in a pub;
be found guilty of rape (boys).
must pay full fare on public transport.

can:
be sentenced to youth custody;
be sent to prison to await trial (boys);
see a category 15 film;
open a Post Office Girobank account although you will need a guarantor i.e. someone who will be liable for your debts.

can: leave school;

get a full-time job and join trade union;

marry with the consent of your parents, the parent who has custody of you if they're separated, your guardian or the court;

leave home with a parent's consent; consent to sex (though sex between men is not legal until 21);

claim supplementary and social security benefits;

drink beer, wine, cider or perry in a pub, hotel or restaurant if you're having a meal;

buy cigarettes or tobacco;

buy liqueur chocolates;

hold a licence to drive a moped, motorcycle, certain tractors and invalid carriages;

buy fireworks and Premium bonds;

enter a brothel and live there;

sell scrap metal;

join the armed forces with your parents' consent (men);

have to pay prescription charges, unless you are pregnant or in full-time education or on a low income or in certain other circumstances;

have to pay for some dental treatment (e.g. a bridge or dentures) unless you are still in full-time education.

choose your own doctor (with parents' consent);

consent to any medical or dental treatment (you can also consent if you are under 16 and understand the implications of what you are doing);

have an abortion without parents' consent;

apply for a passport with the consent of one parent. If you are married or in the armed services you don't need your parent's consent;

be given a community service order if you are convicted of an imprisonable offence;

take part in public performances without a local authority licence.

can:

become a street trader;
join the armed forces with your parents' consent (women) at 17½;
hold a driving licence for all types of vehicles except heavy good vehicles;
be sent to prison;
be made subject to a probation order;
buy or hire any firearm or ammunition;
have an air weapon with you in a public place;
apply for a helicopter pilot's licence,

can:

leave home whether or not your parents agree;
marry without your parents' consent;
join the armed forces without your parents' consent;
vote in local and general elections;
sit on a jury:
get a cheque card and credit card;
see a category 18 film
make a will and act as executor for someone else's will;
give blood;
change your name without your parent's consent;
apply for your own passport without your parent's consent;
buy on hire purchase, get credit and a mortgage;
own land, property and shares in your own name;
sign contracts, sue and be sued in the courts;
buy drinks in pubs and drink them there;
work in a bar;
enter a betting shop and make a bet;
see your birth certificate if you are adopted;
open a bank account or Giro account without your parents' signature;
emigrate without parents' permission;
if you are adopted, you can apply to see your birth certificate.

107

can:

stand for the local council or Parliament; adopt a child; hold a licence to sell intoxicating liquor; be sentenced to life imprisonment if convicted of certain very serious crimes; hold a licence to drive a lorry or a bus.

USEFUL BOOKS AND PAMPHLETS

In addition to the books mentioned at the end of each section in this guide, you may find the following helpful.

Civil Liberty: The NCCL Guide, edited by Thornton, Hurwitt and others; comprehensive guide to the law and your rights (Penguin, 1987, forthcoming)

Make It Happy: What Sex is All About, by Jane Coussins, Easy-to-read, sensible, non-sexist. (Penguin, 1980, £2.95)

Teachers and the Law, by G R Barrell. Legal handbook for teachers on employment law, schools, juvenile court etc. Useful for young people as well as teachers. (Methuen, 1978, £10.95)

Trouble with the Law, The Release Bust Book: practical advice on police powers, courts, lawyers, etc. (Pluto Press, 1987, forthcoming)

Women's Rights: A Practical Guide, by Anna Coote and Tess Gill. Extremely useful guide covering sex discrimination and equal pay, social security, marriage, motherhood, cohabitation etc. Useful for men too. (Penguin, 1981, £3.95)

Rights, Responsibilities and the Law, by Judith Edmunds. This excellent teaching book provides practical practical information on the law and the rights and responsibilities of individuals in modern society. (Thomas Nelson, 1982, £4.65)

SCOTLAND

Your Rights at the Children's Hearings; SCCL; 10p each plus postage.

Your Rights if your Child is in Care; SCCL, 10p each plus postage.

Your Child's Rights to be Educated; SCCL, 10p each plus postage.

The Police, Children's Panels and the Courts; Jordanhill College of Education; £4.50.

The Law and Everyday Life; Jordanhill College of Education; £4.50.

All the Scottish titles are available from Scottish Council for Civil Liberties, 146 Holland Street, Glasgow, G2 4NG.

USEFUL ORGANISATIONS

You can get more information about these organisations, including a list of their publications, by writing to them with a large stamped addressed envelope.

Abortion Law Reform Association 88A Islington High Street, London N1 (01-359 5200); campaigning organisation, does not give advice.

Advisory Centre for Education (ACE) 18 Victoria Park Square, London E2 9PB (01-980 4596)

Advisory Service for Squatters 2 St Paul's Road, London N1 (01-359 8814; hours 2pm-6pm)

Alone in London Service 190 Euston Road, London NW1 (01-278 4225); advice and practical help for single young women and men. Near Euston Station.

Albany Trust 24 Chester Square, London SW1 (01-730 5871); advice on sexual problems.

Al-Anon 61 Great Dover Street, London SE1 (01-403 0888) for relatives of alcoholics.

Alcoholics Anonymous 11 Redcliffe Gardens, London SW10 9 BQ (general enquiries 01-352 9779; practical advice in Greater London: 7 Morton Street, London, SW1, hours 10am-10pm every day of the year; 01-834 8202; for local members, see local phone book)

Amnesty International 5 Roberts Place (off Bowling Green Lane), London EC1R OEJ (01-251 8371); help for prisoners of conscience.

Anti-Apartheid Movement 13 Mandela Street, London NW1 ODW. (01-387 7966)

Apex Trust 31-3 Clapham Road, London SW9 (01-582 3171); helps ex-prisoners find jobs.

Blacks and In Care 20 Compton Terrace, London N1 2UN (01-226 7102)

Black Rights 221 Seven Sisters Road, London N7 (01-281 2340)

British Agencies for Adoption and Fostering 11 Southwark Street, London SE1 (01-407 8800)

110

British Pregnancy Advisory Service Guildhall Buildings, Navigation Street, Birmingham 2 (021-643 1461) or 7 Belgrave Road, London SW1 (01-222 0985)

British Youth Council 57 Chalton Street, London NW1 (01-387 7559); national forum for young people.

Brook Advisory Centre 233 Tottenham Court Road, London W1 (01-580 2991, 01-323 1522); advice and help on contraception, pregnancy, abortion; particularly designed to help young people.

Campaign for Homosexual Equality (CHE) Room 221, 38 Mount Pleasant, London WC1 (01-359 3973)

Campaign for Nuclear Disarmanent 22-24 Underwood Street, London N1 (01-250 4010)

Centrepoint Soho 33 Long Acre, London WC2 (01-437 6394, 01-379 3466); night shelter for people aged 16-25 who are new to London; open 8pm-8am every day.

Child Poverty Action Group 5 Bath Street, London EC1V 9QA (01-242 3225)

Children's Legal Centre 20 Compton Terrace, London N1 2UN (01-359 6251)

Citizens' Advice Bureaux (National Association), 115/123 Pentonville Road, London N1 9LZ (01-833 2181) look in phone book for local CAB

Citizens' Rights Office 5 Bath Street, London EC1V 9QA (01-405 5942); advice and help on social security problems.

Claimants Union 296 Bethnal Green Road, London E2 (01-739 4173)

Commission for Racial Equality 10-12 Allington Street, London SW1E 5EH (01-828 7022)

Consumers' Association 14 Buckingham Street, London WC2N 6DS (01-839 1222)

Department of Education and Science Elizabeth House, York Road, London SE1 (01-928 9222)

Disability Alliance 25 Denmark Street, London WC2 8NJ (01-240 0806)

Equal Opportunities Commission Overseas House, Quay Street, Manchester (061-833 9244)

111

Family Planning Association for Northern Ireland 47 Botanic Avenue, Belfast 7 (0232-25488)

Family Planning Information Service 27 Mortimer Street, London W1 (01-636 7866)

Family Rights Group 6-9 Manor Gardens, London N7 (01-272 7308, 01-272 4231)

Friends of the Earth 377 City Road, London EC1V 1NA (01-837 0731)

Gingerbread 35 Wellington Street, London WC2 (01-240 0953); association for single parent families.

Health Education Council 78 New Oxford Street, London WC1 (01-637 1881); free leaflets on sexual development, VD, drugs, contraception etc.

Terrence Higgins Trust B M AIDS, London WC1N 3XX (01-833 2971); information and advice on AIDS.

Howard League for Penal Reform 320 Kennington Park Road, London SE11 (01-735 3317)

Institute for the Study of Drug Dependence 1-4 Hatton Place, London EC1 (01-430 1991); general information and research on drugs.

International Adoption Society, 160 Peckham Rye, London SE22 (01-693 9611); counselling for single pregnant girls.

International Social Service 39 Brixton Road, London SW9 (01-735 8941); can advise on marriage to a citizen of a foreign country.

Irish Centre 52 Camden Street, London NW1 (01-485 0051); advice and practical help for Irish people in London.

Justice for Children 35 Wellington Street, London WC2; advice for children in care.

Joint Council for the Welfare of Immigrants 44 Theobalds Road, London WC1 (01-405 5527); advice and help on immigration and citizenship problems.

Law Centres Federation Duchess House, Warren Street, London W1 (01-387 8368); can provide a list of local law centres.

Legal Action Group 242 Pentonville Road, London N1 (01-883 2931); can provide list of local law centres.

Lesbian and Gay Switchboard c/o 5 Caledonian Road, London N1 (01-837 7324) 24 hour information and help.

Lesbian and Gay Youth Movement BM-LGYM, London W1 (01-317 9690)

London Housing Aid Centre 189a Old Brompton Road, London SW5 (01-373 7276)

London Lesbian and Gay Centre 69 Cowcross Street, London EC1M 6BP (01-608 1471)

London Youth Advisory Centre 26 Prince of Wales Road, London NW5 (01-267 4792)

Manpower Services Commission Press and Information Office, Selkirk House, High Holborn, London WC1 (01-386 1213); administers job centres and training schemes.

Maternity Alliance 59 Camden High Street, London NW1 (01-388 6337)

Mencap Royal Society for Mentally Handicapped Children and Adults, 123 Golden Lane, London EC1 (01-253 9433)

National Abortion Campaign 70 Great Queen Street, London WC2 (01-405 4801)

National Association of Young People's Counselling and Advisory Services 17-23 Albion Street, Leicester LE1 6GD (0533-554775)

National Association of Young People in Care Rooms 21-22, The Wool Exchange, Market Street, Bradford BD1 1LD (0274-728484) and 20 Compton Terrace, London N1 2UN (01-226 7102)

National Association for the Care and Resettlement of Offenders 169 Clapham Road, London SW9 (01-582 6500)

National Association for Mental Health (MIND) 22 Harley Street, London W1N 2ED (01-637 0741)

National Children's Bureau 8 Wakley Street, London EC1V 7QE (01-278 9441)

National Council for Civil Liberties 21 Tabard Street, London SE1 4LA (01-403 3888); campaigning organisation, can also advise on women's rights, police powers, prisoners' rights, lesbian and gay rights, etc.

National Council for One Parent Families 255 Kentish Town Road, London NW5 2LX (01-267 1361)

National Marriage Guidance Council Herbert Grey College, Little Church Street, Rugby (0788-73241); look in local phone book or contact them for local number; helps couples aged 16 or over, married or not.

113

National Society for the Prevention of Cruelty to Children 1 Riding House Street, London W1 (01-580 8812)

National Union of Students Nelson Mandela House, 461 Holloway Road, London N7 6LJ (01-272 8900)

National Youth Bureau 17-23 Albion Street, Leicester LE1 6GD (0533-554775); research projects and publications about young people.

New Grapevine 416 St John Street, London EC1 (01-278 9147); help with sexual problems of young people

Northern Ireland Civil Rights Association 2 Marquis Street, Belfast (0232 23351)

Police Complaints Authority 10 Great George Street, London SW1P 3AE

Police Staff College Bramshill House, Hartley Wintney, Basingstoke, Hampshire (025-126 2931); prepares reading lists on request, general enquiries etc.

Radical Alternatives to Prison BCM Box 4842, London WC1N 3XX (01-542 3744)

Rastafarian Advisory Service 17a Netherwood Road, Hammersmith, London W14 OBL (01-602 3767)

Release 169 Commercial Street, London E1 6BW (01-837 5602); advice on drugs, abortion, police powers and the courts etc; can refer you to a solicitor.

Rights of Women 52-54 Featherstone Street, London EC1 (01-251 6577); legal advice on women's rights

Royal Scottish Corporation 37 King Street, London WC2 (01-240 3718); advice and help for Scots people in London.

Royal Society for the Prevention of Cruelty to Animals Causeway, Horsham, Sussex, RH12 1HC (0403-64181)

Runnymede Trust 178 North Gower Street, London NW1 2NB (01-387 8943); maintains a library and information service on race and immigration.

Samaritans (London 01-626 9000; look in phone book for local numbers); help for the suicidal and for people with other emotional problems.

Schools Council Newcombe House, 45 Notting Hill Gate, London W11 (01-229 1234)

Scottish Association for the Care and Resettlement of Offenders 53 George Street, Edinburgh 2 (031-226 4222)

Scottish Council for Civil Liberties (SCCL) 146 Holland Street, Glasgow G2 4NG (041-332 5960)

Scottish Council for Single Parents 13 Gayfield Square, Edinburgh EH1 3NX (031-556 3899)

Shelter Housing Aid Centre 189a Old Brompton Road, London SW5 (01-373 7276)

Shelter 157 Waterloo Road, London SE1 (01-633 9377)

Society of Teachers Opposed to Physical Punishment (STOPP) 18 Victoria Park Square, London E2 9PB (01-980 8523)

Standing Conference on Drug Abuse (SCODA) 1-4 Hatton Place, London EC1 (01-403 2341); registry of facilities for drug users.

Trades Union Congress (TUC) Congress House, 23-8 Great Russell Street, London WC1 (01-636 4030)

Ulster Pregnancy Advisory Service 338-338a Lisburn Road, Belfast 9 (0232-667345)

United Kingdom Immigrants Advisory Service 7th floor, Brettenham House, Savoy Street, London WC2 (01-240 5176); advice and help on immigration, citizenship and refugee problems.

Women's Aid Federation England 374 Gray's Inn Road, London WC1 (01-837 9316); co-ordinates women's aid centres for battered women.

Youth Aid 9 Poland Street, London W1 (01-439 8523); research and pressure group especially on training and employment.

Youth Hostels Association (England and Wales) 14 Southampton Street, London WC2 (01-240 3158)

MEMBERSHIP FORM

I/We want to join NCCL

☐ Individual by direct debit £11·50

☐ Individual £12·00

☐ Any two people at the same address £15·00 (£14·50) **by direct debit**

☐ Students, OAPs, claimants £6·00 (or two at same address £10)

☐ Prisoners **£3·00**

☐ I/We have completed the direct debit form

☐ I/We enclose subscription   £_____

☐ I/We enclose a donation   £_____

Total £_____

...am/are not a member/members of any organisation whose objectives are incompatible with those of the NCCL.

Signature(s) _____

Name(s) _____

Address _____

_____ Postcode _____

☐ Please send me more information about NCCL's local groups

☐ Please tell me how to affiliate my organisation to NCCL

☐ Please send me more information about the civil liberties charity, the Cobden Trust

☐ Please send information about the Women's Rights' Fund

*A copy of the constitution is available from NCCL

DIRECT DEBITING MANDATE

Reference Number ☐☐☐☐☐☐☐☐

(for office use)

To: The Manager _____

_____

(Full Postal Address of Your Bank Branch)

Bank Sort Code ☐☐ - ☐☐ - ☐☐

Name of Account to be debited _____

Bank Account Number ☐☐☐☐☐☐☐☐

I/We authorise you until further notice in writing to charge to my/our account with you on or immediately after the

1st of _____ (*) and monthly/quarterly/annually thereafter unspecified amounts which may be debited thereto at the instance of the **National Council for Civil Liberties** (NCCL) by Direct Debit.

Date of first payment on or within one calendar month from _____ (*)

We will enrol you immediately we receive your completed form; the delay in collecting your subscription allows time for our computer and your bank to process your mandate.

Signature _____

Date _____ 19 _____

Banks may decline to accept instructions to charge Direct Debits to certain types of account other than current accounts.

*Please enter the **month after next** here.

After signature, please return this entire form to: National Council for Civil Liberties, 21 Tabard Street, London SE1 4LA. Tel: 01-403 3888

Printed 1986